Inscr
t Elizabeth

SELECTED POEMS

John Frederick Nims,
3-19-86

SELECTED POEMS

JOHN FREDERICK NIMS

The University of Chicago Press
Chicago and London

The University of Chicago Press, Chicago 60637
The University of Chicago Press, Ltd., London

© 1982 by The University of Chicago
All rights reserved. Phoenix edition 1982
Printed in the United States of America

89 88 87 86 85 84 83 82   1 2 3 4 5

Library of Congress Cataloging in Publication Data

Nims, John Frederick, 1913–
  Selected poems.

  Reprint of works originally published 1944–1967.
  Contents: From Five young American poets
(1944)—From The iron pastoral (1947)—From A
fountain in Kentucky (1950)—[etc.]
  I. Title.
PS3527.I863A6   1982   811'.54   81-19820
ISBN 0-226-58117-9   AACR2
ISBN 0-226-58118-7 (pbk.)

DEDICATION: LOVE POEM

My clumsiest dear, whose hands shipwreck vases,
At whose quick touch all glasses chip and ring,
Whose palms are bulls in china, burs in linen,
And have no cunning with any soft thing

Except all ill-at-ease fidgeting people:
The refugee uncertain at the door
You make at home; deftly you steady
The drunk clambering on his undulant floor.

Unpredictable dear, the taxi drivers' terror,
Shrinking from far headlights pale as a dime
Yet leaping before red apoplectic streetcars—
Misfit in any space. And never on time.

A wrench in clocks and the solar system. Only
With words and people and love you move at ease;
In traffic of wit expertly manoeuvre
And keep us, all devotion, at your knees,

Forgetting your coffee spreading on our flannel,
Your lipstick grinning on our coat,
So gayly in love's unbreakable heaven
Our souls on glory of spilt bourbon float.

Be with me, darling, early and late. Smash glasses—
I will study wry music for your sake.
For should your hands drop white and empty
All the toys of the world would break.

from
THE IRON PASTORAL

CONTENTS

From
KNOWLEDGE OF THE EVENING (1960)

ON GROWTH AND FORM

A poem speaks for itself; the poet cannot speak up for it, cannot hover over it like a doting parent, insisting on its beauties in the face of a skeptical world. He may choose to reminisce about how it came to be, but nothing he can say will vouch for its quality.

On growth and form: I expropriate that title from a classic of science, in the hope that there are analogies between the findings of D'Arcy Thompson and the course these poems have taken.

The earliest ones, published in the 1940s, have sometimes been pigeonholed with the "formalism" of that decade. But their origins do not lie there; they lie much further back, near the beginnings of childhood. When my first book was published, I was over thirty; behind it lay two decades of inky endeavor and some hundreds of verses, enough to have inflated several chapbooks and launched them gassily into the welkin. From the time I was five or six, I thought poems were a part of the natural world, as real certainly as the rabbits and collies we kept. The earliest verses of my own which I recall date back to grammar school in the 1920s; they are part of a paean for Charles Lindbergh, who had "conquered the air," as I put it, by flying over

> the vast sea that enshrouds
> Nungesser and Coli, the aces of France,
> Who struggled and perished on old Neptune's
> lance.

Anapestic tetrameter—the basic rhythm varied with iambs, spondees, and an amphimacer. Not that I could have used those words. All the poems I had ever known throbbed with a physical rhythm, had what is called *form*. Form is what I thought poems came into the world with, as plants and animals do. Poets, I might have said if given to such talk, have to be careful about how many feet they put into their lines, just as nature has to be careful about how many feet she puts on her own creatures: six for insects, four for animals, two for the likes of us. I probably would have thought "tetrameter" quite as natural an organism as "quadruped." Nature, producing all of her works in this shape or in that one, perpetually delights in the forms she proliferates. With every new discovery, science seems to confirm her preference. It was Murray Gell-Mann, Nobel laureate in physics, who observed that "if we compare the creation of ideas here [in nuclear physics] to the writing of poetry, then we have to write sonnets, and not free verse." It was a professor of theoretical physics, Paul Davies, who in 1980 marveled at "one of the great mysteries of cosmology": the fact that the universe is highly symmetrical and its expansion isotropic. "Out of all the...chaotic motions with which the universe could have emerged from the big bang, why has it chosen such a disciplined and specialized pattern of expansion?" One's aesthetic preferences cannot be all bad if they are in harmony with the universe.

In caring about form, I was being faithful not to a literary movement of the 1940s, but to the sources of poetry as I felt them in those primal intuitions which are, many poets have felt, the "fountain-light of all our day." It is true that since the 1940s the winds of literary fashion, its gusts and flaws, have shifted more than once, and poems have shifted with them. Those in this book, I think, have not so shifted; some will find in that a sign of independence, others a sign of contumacy toward the spirit of the times. The circumstance, like so much of what I am saying, is only descriptive; it has little to do with any worth they may or may not have as poems.

But if they have not changed much with the times, they have developed—or so a fond parent might believe—in their own way. Among the earliest are many pieces that I now recognize as akin to *Dinggedichte*, or "thing-poems." Often with a local setting, they worked up such themes as a beach in Evanston, a penny arcade in the Loop, one of the south-side movies of my youth, the Chicago El. Most of these I have omitted. Others, written during the war years of the early 1940s, were, like so many war poems, casualties of their war: they are better buried. Is it not true that poems which truckle to their own time rarely survive it?

The stringencies of structure and subject in *The Iron Pastoral* were relaxed in the collection that followed three years later, its emphasis less on the thing observed than on the person observing.

It was not until another ten years had gone by that the next collection, *Knowledge of the Evening*, was ready. Nearly half of that decade had been spent abroad, mostly in Italy and Spain. Some of the poems are set in Europe, but they are not, at least to my mind, globe-trotting poems: one sees with new vision the girls under the elms on Kenwood after he has seen the Lady of Elche, the *kore* in Athens, the ivory dancer in Crete. I had also been reading in and translating from other literatures; it is possible that a fondness for Góngora and the occasional hermeticism of Montale encouraged structures that at times murmured for "More light!" "Old River Road," for one, has been found difficult, though I thought it a simple enough meditation on the Paolo and Francesca theme. "The Mirror," abstruse, maybe, but not abstract, is a parable implying that what we know of an ultimate reality is like what some idiot with a little mirror, prowling the shrubbery around a mighty castle, would learn of the brilliant life within from such glimmers as his glass could catch from chink or louvre.

As far as I could make them so, most of these poems were tight structures, tight in a loose-lipped age, when all things—poems among them—seemed to be falling more and more apart. I liked to think of Ben Jonson, clinking brick on brick. Some of my own bricks, it may be, were glazed ceramic, like the tiles of Andalucía; by choice they intended what Wallace Stevens called the "essential gaudiness of poetry." If they are sometimes flamboyant, so sometimes is our nature and its history; if they are sometimes lavish (or what the critics call "rhetorical"), so too was the Parthenon in its greatest day, before sober time had censored away the saffron, blue, and crimson. To speak so of these poems is not to say they were successful.

Whatever they were, the book that followed seven years later, *Of Flesh and Bone,* was a deliberate contraction toward simplicity. Relishing Jules Renard's observation that "one can say of most literature that it is too long," I decided on new ground rules for this one book: no poem over eight lines, all in the simplest forms available. No literary allusions—though here I fell from grace a couple of times. ("With Fingering Hand" translates a phrase from one of Goethe's *Römische Elegien* in which the poet, in bed with his mistress, taps out hexameters on her back with his fingers as he composes a poem. Anacreon too comes tipsily into the book, and so does a line from Yeats.) Themes were to be the basic ones. The two nouns in the title imply love and death, the immemorial staples of lyric (and sometimes ironic) poetry. Yeats in his sixties could write: "I am still of opinion that only two topics can be of the least interest to a serious and studious mind—sex and the dead." "*Is* there more?" wondered Emily Dickinson in a letter written toward the close of her life, "More than Love and Death? Then tell me its name!"

What I have said has been limited to remarks on growth and form. I have said nothing about the soil these poems grew in, the rain that fostered them, the sun that drew them forth. Nothing about their spirit. Such disclosures must come from the poems themselves. They tell us about that soil, that rain, that sun—about that spirit. If they fail to do so, they say little that is worth our hearing.

FIVE YOUNG
AMERICAN POETS

DOLLAR BILL

The feathered thing of silver-grey and jade,
Her wing with sum and pompous annal spread,
Is strangest bird, world's wonder. Of more than stork
Or dove or jay or any eagle bred.
Her silver eggs explode with wine or milk,
Gardenia, limousine, or firework silk.

Her nature wild. Once captured, not a bird,
Heron nor Persian lark, is fed so fine.
Her Audubon, the banker, stalks and peers
Where audits bloom and grills of commerce twine.
She lives in leather nest or cote of steel.
In city migrates on the armored wheel.

Mallard and teal the fowler downs in fall.
But season is open always for green game.
All weapons used: hand or enchanting hair,
Instructed dice or dynamite or flame.
To pipe of organ some in chapel tread;
Others in alley with a pipe of lead.

Nameless. Her whims of voyage none can track.
Her legend lost; perhaps is charm or curse.
From chaw-stained overall she flutters straight
To the sweet nonsense of a lady's purse.
Wanton with rouge, with blood and beer defiled,
Is loved at Christmas by the snowy child.

She teems in steeple wall, or no bells ring;
In clinic roof, or all the patients die;
She lies with laurel on the captain's head
Or nations fall; their banners leave the sky.
Strange bird. Strange music from the poison breath.
Child of green lovebird and the raven death.

PENNY ARCADE

This pale and dusty palace under the El
The ragged bankers of one coin frequent,
Beggars of joy, and in a box of glass
Control the destiny of some bright event.
Men black and bitter shuffle, grin like boys,
Recovering Christmas and elaborate toys.

The clerk controls the air gun's poodle puff
Or briefly the blue excalibur of a Colt,
Sweeps alien raiders from a painted sky,
And sees supreme the tin flotilla bolt.
Hard lightning in his eye, the hero smiles,
Steady MacArthur of the doodad isles.

The trucker arrogant for his Sunday gal
Clouts the machine, is clocked as "Superman!"
The stunted negro makes the mauler whirl
Toy iron limbs; his wizen features plan
The lunge of Louis, or, no longer black,
Send to the Pampas battering Firpo back.

Some for a penny in the slot of love
Fondle the bosom of aluminum whores,
Through hollow eye of lenses dryly suck
Beatitude of blondes and fallen drawers.
For this Cithaeron wailed and Tempe sighed,
David was doomed, and young Actaeon died.

Who gather here will never move the stars,
Give law to nations, track the atom down.
For lack of love or vitamins or cash
All the bright robins of their year have gone.
Here heaven ticks: the weariest tramp can buy
Glass mansions in the juke-seraphic sky.

MAGAZINE STAND

Here shines the grotto of our lacquered saints.
Their locks are lightning and their eye a knife.
They and the flooded angels who see God
Alone take straight the stinging scotch of life.
They stride the world, gather with magic glove
War's angry garland or the flowers of love.

Here in the urns and roses of the garden,
Her finger in the rites of nicotine,
Beauty is dreaming in her chlorine tresses,
And pastry angels of the cinema lean.
Here Petty's queen, the madonna of the lathe,
Is choired with the naked saints that grin and bathe.

In nickel pots of paper, knighthood flowers:
Cowboys are riled and beautiful with wounds;
Plummet to earth hyena-men from Mars;
The princess in delicious torture swoons;
And a blonde the nazis know with tapping hand
Panics the sanctum of the high command.

A college too: for boys and popeyed scholars
The virgin tables of all knowledge lie,
The roisterous catalogue of sport or sex
And how to dance or in five lessons fly.
For deeper mind, the planets' stolen codes
And what the dragon of the zodiac bodes.

Mont-Saint-Michel of pulp on every corner
Climbing the sky, vermilion, gold, and green,
Is shrine of our ideal and perhaps holy,
The taste of God being wry and absinthe-keen:
His favorite toy the lamb with broken spring;
His favorite singer the adulterous king.

THE GENUINE ELLIS

The soul too is dragged by the body into the region of the changeable, wanders and is confused; the world spins round her, and she is like a drunkard when she touches change—Plato

One thought is all the burden of our learning:
What is and what is not.
For this
The kindergarten shines at first communion
And the slugged goon is shot.
The broker yachts the Florida wave. Slum-fevered
The lungs of lovers rot.

Local Boy, Nine, Swims Lake. Hits Fortieth
    Homer.
Wins All-American Rate.
Condescends to coke, revered; and lolls at many
A moonlit gate.
Desires
One girl—and a highschool teacher marries
That nextdoor date.

A Phi Beta Kappa sops head in a desperate
    ointment;
Is bald as a toad.
Morbid, reads stoic Plutarch, dotes on a razor;
One day
Digs at his throat.
Is alarmed at the speed of blood, swabs iodine, sobbing:
"Hell of a note."

Encircling our Coney shore the waded oceans
Loiter and loot.
And out of sky, abrupt on a pleasant evening,
The riddled airmen chute.
Through autumn of blood advances the lonely
    hunter
With brutal boot.

The dunce world, capped with day, with darkness
    trousered,
Is to this college brought,
To learn:
Love is, or it isn't love, and what is?
Mind errs and flesh is flogged. Passion is taught
To build igloos of the icy cubes of concept,
Ergo and ought.

We, seasick, leap to land from the reeling scupper;
Love sun, being bred of night;
Endure
Our inky earth eclipsed from a sun off somewhere,
Fearfully bright.
Who shall know as we, we duped, the genuine Ellis,
Island of light?

NEW YEAR'S EVE

Midnight the years last day the last
high hour the verge where the dancers comet
(loved water lapsing under the bridge
and blood dear blood by the bridged aorta
where the dreaming soul leans distant-eyed
long-watching the flood and its spoil borne seaward)

and I one fleck on the numbered face
one dot on the star-aswarming heaven
stand here in this street of all our streets
of all our times this moment only
the bells the snow the neon   faces
each our own but estranged and fleeing

from a bar all tinkle and red fluorescence
a boy in a tux with tie uneven
puppy-clumsy with auldlangsyning
plaintive so droll came crying Sally
Salleee again and Saalleee louder
a violin teased   he passed in laughter

yet under the heart of each up vein
up brain and loud in the lonely spirit
a-rang desire for Sallys name
or another name or a street or season
not to be conjured by any horn
nor flavored gin nor the flung confetti

o watcher upover the world look down
through gale of stars to the globes blue hover
and see arising in troubled mist
from firefly towns and the dark between them
the waif appeal from lackland hearts
to Sallys name or perhaps anothers

MADRIGAL IN TIME OF WAR

Beside the rivers of the midnight town
Where four-foot couples love and paupers drown,
Shots of quick hell we took, our final kiss,
The great and swinging bridge a bower for this.

Your cheek lay burning in my fingers' cup;
Often my lip moved downward and yours up
Till both adjusted, tightened, locksmith-true:
The flesh precise, the crazy brain askew.

Roughly the train with grim and piston knee
Pounded apart our pleasure, you from me;
Flare warned and ticket whispered and bell cried.
Time and the locks of bitter rail divide.

For ease remember, all that parted lie:
Men who in camp of shot or doldrum die,
Who at land's-end eternal furlough take

—This for memento as alone you wake.

PARTING: 1940

Not knowing in what season this again
Not knowing when again the arms outyearning
Nor the flung smile in eyes not knowing when

Not sure beyond all doubt of full return
Not sure of time now nor the film's reversal
This all done opposite, the waif regathered

Like our lost parents in the blinded song
We bag in hand with wandering steps and slow
Through suburbs take our solitary way

Not that all clouds are garrisoned and stung
Not that horizons loom with coppered legions
Not that the year is dark with weird condition

All who parted in all days looked back
Saw the white face, the waving. And saw the sea
Not knowing in what season this again

For well they knew, the parters in all evenings
Druid and Roman and the rocked Phoenician:
The blood flows one imposed way, and no other

FROM

THE IRON
PASTORAL

CHRISTMAS TREE

This seablue fir that rode the mountain storm
Is swaddled here in splints of tin to die.
Sofas around in chubby velvet swarm;
Onlooking cabinets glitter with flat eye;
Here lacquer in the branches runs like rain
And resin of treasure starts from every vein.

Light is a dancer here and cannot rest.
No tanagers or jays are half so bright
As swarms of fire that deep in fragrance nest
In jungles of the gilt exotic night
Where melons hang like moonstone. White above
Rises that perfect star, the sign of love.

On carpets' fairy turf, in rainbow dark,
Here once the enchanted children laid their heads,
Reached for the floating moon above the park,
And all their hopes were simple blues and reds.
Beneath the electric halo, none could see
Swords in the ankle of the victim tree.

Each named a patron star: Arthur said green
For August in the country; and Betty blue
For swinging and the Florida surf; while Jeanne
Decided gold. One horoscope was true:
The star of Donald low and lava-red—
Enlisted Donald, in Australia dead.

Our lives were bound to sorcery and night.
Zodiacs crumble on the boughs of rust
For every child is gone. Some burned too bright
And now lie broken in the bins of dust;
And some, a fortunate few, adventured far
And found assurance in the perfect star.

TRAINWRECKED SOLDIERS

Death, that is small respecter of distinction,
Season or fitness, in an instant these
Tan casual heroes, floral with citation,
Scattered for blocks over the track
In lewd ridiculous poses, red and black.

These had outfaced him in the echoing valleys;
Thwarted like men of stone incredible fire;
Like dancers had evaded the snub bayonet;
Had ridden ocean or precipitous air.
Death turned his face aside, seemed not to see.
His unconcern made boyish melodrama
Of all that sergeant threatened, corporal bore,
Or captain shouted on the withering shore.

He watched the newsreel general pinning on their
Blouses the motley segments of renown;
Stood patient at the cots of wounded
Where metal pruned and comas hung;
Nodded to hear their plans: one with a child
His arms had never held; one with a bride;
One with a mere kid's longing for the gang
In green and ticking poolroom bluff with beer.
All these he herded through sargasso of mines
Back to the native field and Sunday steeple
Where only the russet hunters late in fall
Nitre the frosty heaven with abrupt smoke.
There he arose full height, suddenly spoke.

Spoke, and the four dimensions rocked and
    shattered;
Rearing, the olive pullmans spun like tops;
Corridors shrank to stairway and shot up;
Window, green pastoral lately, turned grenade;
The very walls were scissor and cut flesh.
Captain and sergeant tumbled, wholly void
Their muscle, fortitude, and khaki fame
Like rules intended for another game.

Then death, the enormous insolence effected,
The tour de force pat and precisely timed,
Resumes his usual idiom, less florid:
A thousand men are broken at Cologne;
Elderly salesman falters on the landing;
Girl Slain in Park; Plane Overdue; Tots Drown.
But we who walk this track, who read, or see
In a dark room the shaggy films of wreck—
What do the carrion bent like letters spell
More than the old *sententiae* of chance?—
Greek easier (αἴλινον αἴλινον) than this fact.
You lie wry X, poor men, or empty O,
Crux in a savage tongue none of us know.

AIRPORT: IN FOG

When we chipped flint and wore molars and pelts,
Such a sky kept us in rock stalls
Fretting on murky bearskin, while flame
Reddened cartoons of musk-ox on the walls.

Now big men prowl in chromium rotundas,
Inspect flight coupons, compare clock and code;
Would exorcise with voodoo of beam and needle
Spectre of cirrus from the primitive road.

Planes, waddlers on land, all tin and finery,
Grin at the frosted glass of air, abashed.
Actress and banker stare at schedules
Here on the smallprint of terse weather dashed.

Our blood remembers rock, orange cartoon.
Sniffs in best linen the bearskin bed.
If hatchet fall, if superjet, blood shows
—On chromium or flint—identical red.

MIDWEST

Indiana: no blustering summit or coarse gorge;
No flora lurid as disaster-flares;
No great vacuities where tourists gape
Nor mountains hoarding their height like millionaires.
More delicate: the ten-foot knolls
Give flavor of hill to Indiana souls.

Topography is perfect, curio-size;
Tidy as landscape in museum cases.
What is beautiful is friendly and underfoot,
Not flaunted like theater curtains in our faces.
No peak or jungle obscures the blue sky;
Our land rides smoothly in the softest eye.

Man is the prominent fauna of our state.
Elsewhere circus creatures stomp and leer
With heads like crags or clumps. But delirious nature
Once in a lucid interval sobering here
Left (repenting her extravagant plan)
Conspicuous on our fields the shadow of man.

FOTO-SONNETS

Provincetown

Over studded wharves and timber alleys
Gulls in the keen heaven cry like cats;
Trellis of rope, nest of twittering pulleys
Shadow the copper brine of rotund vats.
Ocean is spectra-colored now at noon:
Bronze in the shallows, casing weed or spoil;
Plum at edge of sky or freckle dune;
Under the piling, heavy-green as oil.

The hours go by like avenue girls at Easter—
But time is briny, booted, with cut hands.
Seamen in orange plaid and leathery master
Clump barrel-footed on the creaking sands,
Curse, clamber, haul and tauten, gamble, die,
Caught in the flashing scissor, wave and sky.

Cape Cod

Here is the postcard land on every side:
Each shutter on the undulant shingle poses;
Over camel dunes and ice-blue tide
The cumulus hangs unfolding like white roses.
Each corner of the sky a flourish of gull
Motifs; each bay a boat with canvas steeple;
Up alleys peaked and shingled, louvered tall,
Wander in skipper togs amphibious people.

Men of the umber flats or obstinate highlands,
Grudge nothing: photo lustre is paper-thin.
Schooners go down among the summer islands;
Each village knows the graveyard's stony grin.
These men are fellow in fate: skimp, suffer, plan,
Limp with the abrupt dignity of man.

Waterfront Cafe

The candles shine in bottles rough with wax.
No other light in the long cross-timbered room
Cumbered with gear of voyage: oars on racks,
Seines, pulleys, anchors tangle in the gloom.
No other light, except the orchid panes
Dripping and crowded with the twilit ocean;
No sound except pressure like many rains;
Except the wick's compass of air, no motion.

Fonder of smiles than phrases, olive girls
Carry in steam honest tureens of chowder,
In corners where they walk candlelight whirls
And shadows wheel around; merriment's louder:
Murmur of gesturing sailor and his date
And tinkle of silver on the careless plate.

Stunted Fir

Inland, the region of stunted fir.
A sinewy cripple, grim, with knotted stare;
Its bark abrupt with turtle-shell and spur

And rough with quills of porcupine for hair.
Wailing on every dune, the angry clan
Clutches debris in fingers ash and wry.
Its posture dear to colorist of Japan,
It shakes a shaggy lustre on the sky.

Sardonic too, bearing for fruit or blossom
Its crude repeated hoax, the wooden cone.
Men buy it as oddity (life playing possum?),
Tack it on wall, with cane and pennant shown,
Or knotted in cocoa vines and rocks
Hang it in ornate jungle of cuckoo clocks.

Return

From pines, andirons of the fuming sea,
Reluctantly we part, like cordage tearing,
Wrapped in tatters of salt memory
Angry as pennons in this weather flaring.
Wanting, through lenses of the pendulous tide,
The raggedy hardware of the ocean floor;
Wanting the dunes of autumn, easel-pied,
And shack of painter jaunty on the shore.

Back to the shuttle country, sheer New York,
We carry the tourist's flotsam, cards and flags,
Bayberry candles and the floats of cork
(Shreds of the great peninsula in bags)
And tangled with kelp and hawser, hardly whole,
Haul like a net our green and driftwood soul.

AFTERSONG

The night of mouth to mouth
Dissolves in the rainy morning.
Breath is unknotted from breath;
Heart from its best home torn.

What flotsam flickers away
In the gutter nodding and sombre?
Hollows under the knee
And the breast right size of palm.

Great heavens crumple and droop;
The room with the shy door closes.
O kisses, sea-awash cup!
Rain over bramble and rose.

A FOUNTAIN IN KENTUCKY

THE MASQUE OF BLACKNESS

The first face of the Scene *appeared all obscure,*
& nothing perceiu'd but a darke Rocke, with trees beyond
it; and all wildnesse, that could be presented; Till, at one
corner of the cliffe, aboue the Horizon, *the* Moone
began to shew . . .

I

The news stirred first in very dead of winter:
A rumor of new breathing by late spring,
New lungs for the world's air, planets' new center,
New eyes brimming new colors—a new everything!
The ticking kaleidoscope rearranged its tenses;
The present faded; future's the true noon.
As both the man and woman grew new senses
They laughed at sun, set all their dials by Soon.

The streets and rooms they moved in rang unreal
Since not yet real to the child; say someone's dream
Strange as drowned cities where the cursive eel
Flashes in alleys. A curtain-time scene:
Whether they shifted vases, turned a page,
All seemed last-minute touches on a stage.

II

The stage and a man's life—long before Avon
Cynical Palladas saw we "play a part."
Though of that scenery or the gapes it gave on—
Hard to say which is model and which art.
Down the steep aisles of a murky vast
Theater, all seats empty, he and she
Go groping backstage; from a passionate past
Glitter the lurid flats of cloud and sea.

On one dark door a blurred name and a star;
Many costumes: banker, burglar, streaming sheik;
Many props: sword, castle, couch, arrogant car,
High enough balconies to break a neck.
He sits down, a most "practicable" bed;
She feels a dagger and the edge runs red.

III

Up with the drowsy curtain! No more slumber—
Hear the telephone dinning at midnight in the west?
The far-off hospital nudging his number:
The baby is born sooner than they guessed.
O thousand miles of wire, you may well be humming
To tractors and farms and fences and silos and
   signboards and, well,
Say to those huddled towns, say: Someone's coming:
Out with your bunting; bang on that firebell.

But in deserted halls of the long dorm
Corners piled with luggage jostle and sigh.
The window faint in lightning is breathing warm.
And look: pandemonium in the sky
As moons (a trick of tears) are bobbing in tens;
Each star is twenty stars! What a wild lens!

IV

In the cradle, furled, unfurled, anemone fingers
Stir celluloid susurrus and pink chime;
How they shall hook *him* where he brags and lingers,
Old mustache-tugging, flint, foreclosing Time.
Let him rasp let him grin let him wheedle:
   must disgorge.
Palms must twist up, slow-open tense as traps
Restoring coins, curls, girls in the Greek surge,
And tears that fell pitting forlorn war-maps.

Then yours (anemone) rain-wandering panes
All joy at dusk; the Magi's intense shed;
Skill with a knife, decision, trucks and cranes;
Tall midnight prodding many a guess at God—
That love that moves the sun. From love you are;
O plunge unaging in the enraging star!

V

A six-month-old discoverer, this baby
Goggles for days at his elate right hand
Till his head falters and blue eyes blur. Maybe
He gurgles an off-vowel sound, nodding bland.
Then the hand hovers, sways like a pink flower—
What will you do with it turned brusque and human?
Half floral and half bird no more—tweed power,
Wristwatch-consulter and cigared acumen?

On keyboard, dashboard, surfboard, labor-relations
    board
O use it better than we, your likely future:
Manage for human hope earth's pirate hoard
And trick the tumblers of combustible nature.
Or, mildlier made, project us. Call desire
Two cups on midnight throw-rugs by the fire.

VI

One day they learned that sorrow wore old tweed,
That lounging disaster spoke a soft hello.
Not where the wounds of wreck or battle bleed
But in the dullish office you all know.
Many searchlights locked and rusted on that scene
Throw blacker shapes than noon: there the child lies;
Doctors are curt, averted; what they mean
Concern shows livelier in the mother's eyes.

In her tight fingers round a rubber lamb
She brought to show them all: See he can play.

Now if calamity with his drunkard's aim,
Or grief with minimizing hands—if they
Edge up or shriek in the shrubs—no gasp, no start:
This is one routine they know by heart.

VII

Confronting that fact's what-about-it shrug
In a mist of danker friends and family,
They started to take metaphor like a drug,
To lay on open wounds emollient simile.
As: tears are the best lens for seeing sky,
Or: that bluesteel thunder clears the air.
But when alone they sobered, eye to eye,
The big skywriting withered, wasn't there.

What was? Why some irrelevance and flummery:
They noted eyes blurred less in blurring rain,
That cheeks flushed in the snow at least—in summary
Though past and future's gone, some Now remains.
No mountain blazing candid, no, not one—
They picked up pebbles and these argued stone.

VIII

(Antimasque)

Because someone was gone, they bought a dog,
A collie pup, black, orange, flashy white.
He gnawed on table legs, troubled the rug;
His growls and pokings varied the empty night.
Except for that red flopping tongue, a fawn.
Intense but scattering, coffee-eyed. At play
White as piano keys on the green lawn
His paws improvised snatches of ballet.

(The grinning show that Must Go On; the voice
Without past, without future, crying rejoice.)

This dog, this gawk, this zealot of frivolity,
Bounding assiduous sniffer hung with hair—
What could a romping fetish of this quality
Do in that house, with that shadow there?
Oh nothing. They knew that. The insane dancer
Was queried: Dance Dance was all the answer.

IX

One day they made the abandoned beach their home
—The sky electric-blue, sea dark as plum—
And watched the ivory spindles of the foam
Shaped by curved chisels and a big windy thumb.
They loved it here, and would have—none of that!
Rusty with sand the near-in waves grate *no;*
The folly-printed shore utters *no* flat;
Wave erasing wave erasing wave shakes *no.*

   (Above, the clouds' untidy pompous scrawl
   Means *no* if it means anything at all.)

More *no's* flurry the mind than gulls that view.
He stared till italics teased him in the spray
(This lettered man), saw waves scrawl *W*
Stubbornly, turning *no* to *now;* saw *K*
In caving slant of breakers. New winds blow:
With every *K* imploding, *now* was *know.*

X

Know? But know what? Addenda from such minus?
Any true time from clock hands so bent back?
A city from ruins—
Once crystal halls now staring hollow and black?
Two cups all seesaw splinters, telephone's tremor,
Hard Time foreclosing on what appeared free?—
As (almost obscene memento of summer)
A white dog dances by the terrible sea.

Well, they know this: the cloud-ornate proscenium
Where Space-Time whirs a gilt rococo cage
With clowns and cats performing—no millennium
Here. They observed from many-roped backstage
And clanking cellarage. But admired much art,
Seeing the works of the bright world apart.

CITY DAWN

Breath of dawn, that corroborates all fable:
All we wanted in fairytale, is true.
Remember the scene: squires Maying under the
    pennoned castle?
Grass is that green, heaven that storybook-blue.

No domes of Mecca here, those rainbow bubbles.
No tricks of Gothic lightning amazing the sky.
But families live in the clouds, and Sunday pavements
Broader than ballrooms of any Louis lie.

Or is it not steel, not stone, but our own blood
Filling these shapes, as air the vivid balloon?
Raising the intricate skyline miles away,
Floating even the sun toward hover of noon?

Over coffee and fruit such assurance of power
That the heart and the tear ducts choke: too much
    delight—
Returned to the world of solids and positive tread
After the howling mirrors, the chutes and loons of
    the night.

Though the morning paper cry black and squarely Woe
As planes lock, senators jangle, cottages bobble in flood,
There gathers a joy that is not quite lost all day
As we prove *to be, to know* in our warm blood.

THE INDOLENT DAY

Today went meaningless as music.
Variations in the key of rain.
Even the street of hard curbs and porches
Sang in the whirling and pour of the pane.

Was scherzo in the dime-store red as a fire truck.
In the park was adagio and dripping green.
Sloshed in the rubble alley, aqua funebre.
Gasped sostenuto at any machine.

Having all day no wisdom weighed or spoken,
A sheepish no-good I lie alone,
My veins a-humming still like violin strings,
A fife or froggy bassoon in every bone.

Exulting: it might have had other relations and
    intervals,
Been in some exotic scale and not this one
Of affectionate Re, green Mi, history of Sol-fa
Twined in the minor rain, the dominant sun.

A QUIET NIGHT

Eyelids: their petal-on-pond sweet meeting at night.

At once the landscape loosens, flies apart:
On shaggy wing the crow-dark hemlocks shrug,
Flap off in wind; great woods stream to the stars.
Night sees the air fantastic with hunched cows,
Plum freightcars, little spotted dogs. The whirlwind
Zooms it up to a zenith point. There vanished.
Only, beneath bare heaven, a kind of sea heaves.

Then our white torso in dark water awash,
Lost figurehead, limbless, mere driftwood dreaming,
Companioned by tall antlers of wreck, nuzzled
By fish with keys and photographs for scales.

Let the eye flicker—furore shakes the void.
A speck in heaven, exploding, funnels out
Assorted infinity: crow-flapping firs
Desperate for earth, wheelbarrow, blown marquee.
Great sailing planks and parasols, fruitstands
Swirl down in a cyclone, sort themselves, assemble.

When the eyes open, limbs lie make-believe;
Eyes see the room just poised, its curtains breathless;
Out windows see a landscape tense in tableau,
The smallest thing in place (look, the child's cart
With a limp doll grinning in it)—or if not quite,
Inference of night wind, a rumor of rain.

WATCHER GO DEFTLY

Careful, careful; you cannot be too deft
With the pines on the shore and the little shells
Lip-color, eyelid-color, pale as a thigh—
Feel your palm tingle with little gourds and bells?

Especially you are dumb brother seaweed's keeper;
Nobody likes him—clutch, a rubber glove.
This, and all moon-crater gates of crawfish
Look at with love.

Curious chain mail of atoms underfoot,
Pandora's box too fine for fumbling—much
Of this you can penetrate, being careful
With that combustible touch.

But all those girls that kneel to collect shells,
Then straighten, thin girls, swinging back their hair,
That soft explosive fire. Watcher go deftly,
Is there in earth or heaven enough care?

43

FIRST DATE

Her toe first in that water
To which all walkers come
(Not Charon his blunt ferry
Creaks with more travelers home)
She stands, gasping in moonlight,
Never again the same.

Never the girl her mother
Patted pink-ribboned to school;
Never the pet her father
Pleased once with a doll.
And the herons and pines of the picnic beach
Shrink to a small role.

Soon the white ankle, Sharon,
Soon, dear, the nice knee
Tingle and chill, go under—
Then you begin to know.
The dark waves wash to your waist and
Ah there is no help now.

The mottled sand. Two heelprints
Pooling in moonlight there.
A gleam, in the dark we stare on
—Swimming arms? or a star?
Colored lanterns blink on the dune.
Undertow by the shore.

JAPANESE PRINTS

These took the captain prisoner that took these.
He had blown their homes ramshackle as their
   writing is,
Found in the rubble this book, opened it—
In storm clouds, a blue porthole on serenity.

The two-inch craftsmen, intense ivory faces,
Worked in their beamed and linen-colored courtyards:
The bender of bows with his long black
   bow-shaped mustache;
Weavers (two women watched, their intricate hair
Like crullers lacquered); the old utensil-maker,
Pots all around—that picture clanked and glimmered.

Pictures: lenses. See more seeing less,
Seeing this page the sky blows. So this soldier
Took Japan with him, knew his heart Japan:
Japan first pointed his own street and people.

THE WEEDS

By the hot hedge of August these were nothing,
Were nothing in the faddish trees of May.
But now in January this copper garden
Holds fête-champêtre day,

Glum mercury under his glassy ladder sulking.
The fields are lacquer of ice.
Only the waist-high straggle of roan weeds
Extravagant and precise:

One like the peacock's tail imitated in brass;
One with its quarter-inch roses, moth-miller hue;
One like a sepia photo of fireworks; one
Pale-blue as twirl of tattoo.

How could they but be all energy, whorling and torque
Who have survived December trumpeting by;
And bent from the pole star seen, night after night,
White-hot constellations warping the sky?

If barometers told time, these endured epochs.
When all the floe loomed verdant, these were there;
Saw the Green Age itself, unthinkable summer—
These fossils vised in the angry quartz of air.

INCIDENT

Our cinder kitten with violet eyes
Yesterday crept under couches, wouldn't be seen.
At dawn she was dead by the door.

The event was petty; its impetus not.

The orange setter paws her; rearing snorts,
Mills off wild as a wagon-wheel broke loose.

We who this first winter far from town
Walk in the ornate snow and love each other,
Sensible people, never weep for kittens
(Their wide-eyed acrobatics up the banister;
Their witty meetings with rubber mice).

But wading this afternoon in upblown drift
By the lank fences, each one hides
What he hopes the other has not seen: conjecture's
Ragged feather bloodied in the snow.

WINTER IN THE PARK

Lagoons are shrunk and walkable as concrete,
The little islands accessible now
That in June were a green secret the sunburnt lovers
Bumped with their rented prow.

Trees empty and fibrous, as if their roots were in air
By the sidewalk burled with ice
Where concessions huddle boarded, nothing to sell.
Oh how it was shady and nice

In easy July, in the ice-cream days, the lazy
Lying in sunhot grass we two;
The creak and bobble of rowing, the dusty scuff
And stare in the barbarous zoo:

Where lions lay bearded like Holbeins and polar
    bears clowned;
Where Jumbo waved sousaphone trunk;
The black leopard circled in whirlwind with
    flashlight for eyes;
Kangaroos hopped erotic and drunk.

Ape, tiger, swan (child's graphic A B C)
Spelled *us* then, spelled our rage and play.
Now the violent nursery is numb under snow;
The playthings all put away.

VICARAGE BLUES

I was not aboard when the big boat sunk;
I was not in the overturned car.
But I stood on the bank, I stood on the curb,
Frozen for those who were

Till chairs were floating around my neck;
I was upside down in the car.
Men on the shore and the curious curb—
None could think of a cure.

Many a coral girl on the boat;
Many a boy in the car.
As mother, mentor, motorman watch
Ended is all that care.

Ended the blanket tucked at night;
The songs of the caroling car.
Life that flushed as an apple once
Shatters white to the core.

Treasure of curl on the luxury boat;
Treasure of arm in the car.
Night and day dice it away—
Carol and coral and cure.

TWO CRETAN VIEWS

Crete, forty centuries ago.
An afternoon like yesterday
Where, in the mazes of blunt brick,
Sun on the jigsaw gardens lay.

And Minos under a pink and lime
Windy canopy yawned at ease,
Laughed as his cup-chill fingers drew
A girl's white throat to his sunburnt knees.

Minoan boys in the court below
Flashy as dancers, forelocks blown,
Tease a red lackadaisical bull—
Vaulting sharp pendulums of bone;

One eye on the tall girls, two or three,
Who, walking a fawn, laugh taunting praise,
Bright lips arching the kiss-shape cry
(For thick with theta the Cretan phrase).

Servants conduct through the halls
With bull and acrobat glazed
A tiptoeing stranger, wary of eye
In that rumble of corridors—amazed.

A shipwrecked man from the dour north
Where indigo rocky headlands jut—
Forearm corded, salt with the oar,
Craggy of forehead, taut of gut;

A swarthy imaginative man,
That, frozen, stares through a hoarse door
At twisted limbs' contortion in air,
Flaring snout of the Mino-taur,

A rustle of maidens pale in shade,
Red tassels shook from a wild horn.
Fiercely he breaks and flees.
So the great bugaboo is born.

FAIRY TALE FOR MARION

This is the hero; he is black or white,
Jewish or not-chosen, as you will.
He is villain too; porch-pillared from moonlight
And fondling with stub thumb the window sill.

Night wind laps back his hair; why, you all know him.
Eye a little pale, a yes-sir, no-sir mouth.
Disliked his heavy-hand pa, just to show him
Ran away from high school once down south.

He brings the laundry, brown purse a foot wide;
He rattles garbage cans, taxies you home.
Once when in rain you let him step inside
He looked beyond you to the living room.

Eyes narrowed, he hates *come* and *do* and *carry*.
Prince am I none, he feels, yet princely born.
Some stories read when he was ten and scary
Hard upon Shaftoe and the crumpled horn

Expressed him maybe; he didn't know; forgot them
Glowering and drew secret maps in class.
Squirrels chuckled at him and by god he shot them.
His dreams have brought him here and cut this glass,

Or not his dreams. The imprisoned lady rather,
Her snow-white forearms bound, gazed and he came.
Gracious and golden-haired, unlike his mother.
Her hands were like his mother's just the same—

Not that he knew. He only knew the window
Tilted and stuck. Impatient, his blood cursed.
But his two secret words conjured the window.
He thought a moment, swung his left leg first.

Once in, he heard them breathing. Slow, excited,
Clasping her image he made for their den.
A nervous click, the door rushed at him lighted,
All lamps and glass and draperies, the woman

Bolt-upright, unbelieving. He came closer.
The ogre snored beside her, red mouth deep;
Disguised (as always) like Duffy the grocer,
He lay enchanted in a beery sleep.

And threshed and gurgled as the good scout-knife
Cut in, cut deeper and the skin spread wide.
"She is half free," he thought "this saves my darling."
And now for that witch-woman by his side.

53

But slow, but soft; this is liturgy. Once more
He saw the lady beckon, one arm free.
He flung back curtains, found the secret door;
Crooned as he swung it with the golden key.

The deacon two streets over under his steeple
Is dreaming this; his grating molars groan;
It runs with many faces through the people;
Dali will paint it with live telephones.

For this prince saw the ogre red and still;
Killed the enchantress (this was not *his* word);
A fountain of plumes, mounted the glass hill
Led by white reindeer and a silver bird.

Later, in alleys crouched, he never winces
As wheels skid shrieking, men shout, sirens wind.
A prince, he turns his back, smiles at the princess,
And both ride off together down his mind.

PORTRAIT

Seeing in crowded restaurants the one you love
You wave at the door, tall girl in imperious fur,
And make for him, bumping waiters, dropping a glove,
Arriving soft with affectionate slur.
As ladies half-turn, gazing, and men appraise
You heap the linen with purse, scarf, cigarettes, lighter,
Laughing some instantaneous droll phrase.
As if sudden sun came out, the table is brighter.

All moods: at a party everybody's delight;
Intent while brown curls shadow the serious page;
When people are stuffy (more correct than right)
The stamp and turn on heel of a little girl's rage.
But woman mostly, as winter moonlight sees,
Impetuous midnight, and the dune's dark trees.

THE CHILD

How the greenest of wheat rang gold at his birth!
How oaks hung a pomp in the sky!
When the tiptoeing hospital's pillowy arms
Godsped him in suns of July.

Then dizziest poplars, green-and-white tops,
Spun spinning in strings of the wind,
As that child in his wicker
With two great safeties pinned

Slept twenty-two hours with a Buddha-fine face
(His hands were palm-up like a dancer's).
Or his tragic mask's sudden pink-rubbery woe
Sent us thumbing four books for the answers.

And the grave clouds smiled over,
Smiled, flowing west to east, countering sun;
Fields at their leaving all spurted up green!
Old fences limped by at a run!

O elms, fling up up up corinthian fountains.
Fields, be all swirl and spangle: tangle of mirth—
Soon you will root in his woodbrook eyes more deeply
(O reborn poplars) than in Michigan earth.

"HUMAN KIND CANNOT BEAR
VERY MUCH REALITY"

Hence tricks of dimension on us soft as kisses;
Vagueness of towns seen from a little way;
Tact of the hillside oak, giant that presses
Mild on the eye, a feather of grey.

Hence the world rushing down fast from the plane.
In ten seconds Gulliver's toy, its human places
Amusing and trim: no room for the cripple's grin at
    the pane,
The men swinging jagged beerbottles, blood on
    their faces.

Hence tininess: sizzle of distance right in our palm.
What saurians horny with glass the dewdrop carries
Microscope moonlight shows. Or teeming loam—
Black brutes for our safety seen as from forty stories.

Hence too the fortunate limits of love,
Indifference, tedium, pride. Else, carefree and tall,
What man on the lunch-hour street freely could move,
So dumfounded in love with the plain least girl of all?

CHRISTMAS

They say: but cattle near
And the infant in harsh hay!
Indeed harsh: how could honest God
Be man another way?

By lying lax in gold
Near many a bent knee?
Bedded in bright percent and so
Vouching hypocrisy?

Oh man's-flesh is most really this:
A thin cry in the cold;
Dust made a little while aware,
Shriveled both young and old.

When infants are born rich
The gaudy zoos troop in:
The elephant with button eyes;
The tiger, springs of tin.

And friends and relatives gape,
A simple clucking clan.
More honest—no?—when Bethlehem
Told the home-truth of man.

ADAM'S BALLAD

"So sweetly bedded in Being,
So lost in locks of the sun;
So flushed and dazzled by dawn, by
Dark so troubled and spun.

"Bold in the owner's region,
I who have no right here
Have taken Being, his lady,
Slept with his wayward dear.

"Drunk the shy mist, her kisses,
On her wild breasts floated, the sea,
As heaven, bluest eye burning,
Was bending only on me.

"Part of his white love's body
God shall not have again.
He let me in and I took her.
She will stay among men.

"Even God, beholding bright Esse,
Trembles in rage of delight.
What of me, who fast in her forearms
Share the deep of the night?"

Thus as the blood rose warmer
Was Adam's saga begun—
So sweetly bedded in Being,
So lost in locks of the sun.

KNOWLEDGE
OF
THE EVENING

THE LOVER

The lover of many women in his time
Came to his time: the lap of earth uncloses.
"The true to none?"—with sorrow—"true to none
In the long handsome June of all my roses?"

The lover, faint with pain (death's nuclear flash
Had bared the chambers of his life before him,
Seedy resort hotel with two walls gone,
Beds on all fours and trailing laundry) bore him

Like one assured of sympathy—his ear
So cunning in all cadence of surrender.
His famous smile, the "eternal boy's," began;
His famous wistful shrug. The tone less tender:

"Much from an ancient fate. But not your doom.
Your doom is your conceit of what you are.
Violet-stained, in a white fire of lenses,
Your heart become its will: the cancerous star."

His hell began, a hissing of cold foliage.
Hell too much like Eden. A second glance
Showed in the brush a dozen Eves coquetting—
The country club on nights of the spring dance

Had such mysterious tussle in the shrubbery,
Ruby on velvet hushed, from owl to lark.
But here light hugged the turf, a lunar neon
Of taverns known. The dozen brows were dark.

The enchanted wood exhaling fogs of brandy:
Breasts candlelit, a dream of altars, swim.
Knees like the noble jewels that shaft a chalice.
And cloth of gold about the seraphim.

Fingers beckoning like hands on harpstrings.
Shoulders that ebb consenting. Sweetness choked
His heart in the old vice; he fell sobbing
"Thank God!"—the words sprung jackknives
    in his throat.

Two ankles shone like lotus; he flopped toward them
—Half-blinded seal—and spangled them with kisses.
And so kissed up and up in a long whinny
And shivered as he prayed and all delicious.

Kissed to the pulsing throat. Then knew his hell.
A face like a bland egg: no lips to murmur
The summer storm, wet eave, or wishing well.
No breath—perfumed Andalucía—yearning.

No human eye: affectionate fern to ring
Woodland pools the ivory bather haunted.
Lovely: hover of heaven, starlit while
The braw boar in the bracken lashed and grunted.

One hope: ears, sensitive orchids of all music—
To drown his grief in comfortable hair.
Fearful, his fingers sought beneath the tresses—
Howled. And a viper of lightning hissed the air.

OLD RIVER ROAD

i

One party of that season. Evening journals
Whirred to their perch oblivious of doom.
The two reposed their coats. Flanked on a sofa
Sat innocent of the other. Chaffed the room

Till hands by chance encountering in cashews
(Roaming a moment from their tutor eyes)
Touched. And a current flowed. The two were dazzled:
Their hands! to play such lightning from the skies

As rocked impeccable homes to their foundation,
Loosened a promise and shook plaster down,
Baited that pack, the chaste uncharitable
Tongues till they bred contagion about town.

What matter tongues? What matter to the blinding
Mask of agony what the chorus bays?
Touched. And he doffed the satin visor: met her
Delft and undecipherable gaze

Much like the morning spangled in his lashes.
What of the brow's sereneness? Or the hair
Cool and amused, remembering crowns her fervor
Burned to the smoky gold of autumn air?

What of her gaze the gala night deciphered
Pondering mottoes of the barbarous dart?

Thanks to the ash on his lapel consulted
And the false candor of a sinking heart?

Eyes in the other's gloried like plumes tossing
That more and more sang *morituri* plain.
So gladiators in their clanking bonnet
Planting their sandals on the arrogant stain,

Eyes like coals in a great brazier glowing
Around and round the impending thousands scan,·
Seizing the noon for omen! Hola, lobo!
Bloat on the rich disaster if you can.

ii

Both overfrank. In part to trip suspicion,
Part for that dragging mantle, laissez-faire,
Part for the gin, like sacred lamps attended,
They feigned embrace. A spectacle, the pair.

Anon, his tail between his legs, discretion
Deserted these, to mutter among drunks.
A spectacle of some concern to husbands,
Bumbling men unbudgeable as trunks;

Of some concern to keepers of the linen,
Bleak with the blue mondays of the past.
Their keys a-jangle: moon-resistant, May-proof.
Oh that candor were as season-fast!

Laocoön, you would have winked to see them.
Laocoön, out Lackawanna way?
Wrapped in their own bright spirals of endearment
And much aspersed by yodellers. Break of day

Found them the worse for friendly wear: a huddle
Baroque and dowdy, on a jumble of knees.
A hoyden skirt the merciful amended.
The indecent dead are howling rites like these.

Her face a sleepy flower. A child's in fever.
Once in a strange forest long ago
The birds, a shimmer of cocktail hues, came loosing
Leaves where the lost children slept below

As mist impearled the conifers. The matted
Lashes of both the tears enchanted fast.
Delicate: a rare flying thing, its lacy
Wings in the gold collodion of the past.

The tears were hard to pardon. Much-forgiving
Spouses protested water into wine.
But tears are tears. The two had each a reason:
Early morning, and the day's decline.

iii

Brave words at first: the night of nine auroras
Rooting in curious forms of fern and wood

Chanced on a thing of earth the astonished lovers
Had scrupled to imagine if they could.

Angels beckoning Adam to the garden
Shaped with their fingers, flaming, what they meant:
Fuddled the lost lovers with indulgence
No will of theirs had ventured to invent.

They spurned the bogus bloom, cadaverous waxes,
Gathering what abounded and no more.
Stung with no iron glove the face of heaven,
Come to this pretty pass at heaven's door.

But candors flashed, admissible in marble;
Marble darkened with considerate blood;
Blood was a raging main; the embattled galleon
Toppled doubloons and javelins in the flood

As the foam scrolled: Finale. A quick curtain.
Gawky, the room and furniture trooped in.
They sagged in their embrace, strait-jackets giving;
Human heads a-loll with dingy grin.

Breath on the lip, so debonaire a spender
It left the lung no penny of its own,
Shrunk. They felt the hollow in those gaudy
Breasts that festoon the musty coops of bone.

The hollow between heartbeats; looming lobo
Hard on the heels of valor in the snow.

—What of the bright balloon, heaven's effervescence?
Trodden on fairgrounds when the wagons go

To the next town, indifferent, leaving rutted
Yesterday's joy, the fields of pleasure torn.
Where the white queens performing—swans of
  heaven!—
Swooned on their buoyant pole. Like twins unborn

The lovers huddle. Glittering wings that weave
Robes of the forest for our sons and daughters,
Lap them in love, who shrivel as they wait
Numbly, a spirit moving on the waters.

  iv

We are that key the fugitive finger leaves
As soaring gloria stumbles and recovers;
Chords for the Astra Khan roll kansas-black
Packing a violet fire for hidebound lovers.

Lightning: a lifeline between two and heaven
(September's not more pendulous on its stem).
Give the mad gleeman scope; the tarns of Auber
Foster a lotus moon for even them.

We knew one night the neighborhood was shaken,
Explosions underground: till two and two
The sleepers in their crazyquilt, leaves bleaching,
Mushroomed up. As broken springs would do.

Jack in his proper box. But in the pulpit?
Candor in crow or lobo, duck and drake?
An old wives' tale, remember? And what draughtsman
Caught for his rule the wrist-enchaining snake?

But even these! Her footfall shy and naked
Full on the arrogant stain as javelins rang:
A nine-days' leer to shoeclerks who live crouching,
Immaculate dentists catering to fangs.

These meant a noble fitt, but tripped on Aleph
Crooked as rails where ploughing trains collide.
And saw too much in a wrong season. Others
Suffer their trouble late, as saucers ride

Harrowing sky. The Angel of Death in heaven
(Lunatic sunrise in the dead of night)
Sows in our fallow face the ash of roses.
Dust in the eye's a charm for seeing right.

THE YOUNG IONIA

If you could come on the late train for
    The same walk
Or a hushed talk by the fireplace
    When the ash flares
As a heart could (if a heart would) to
    Recall you,
To recall all in a long
    Look, to enwrap you
As it once had when the rain streamed on the
    Fall air,
And we knew, then, it was all wrong,
    It was love lost
And a year lost of the few years we
    Account most—
But the bough blew and the cloud
    Blew and the sky fell
From its rose ledge on the wood's rim to
    The wan brook,
And the clock read to the half-dead
    A profound page
As the cloud broke and the moon spoke and the
    Door shook—

If you could come, and it meant come at the
    Steep price
We regret yet as the debt swells
    In the nighttime
And the *could come, if you could* hum in
    The skull's drum
And the limbs writhe till the bed
    Cries like a hurt thing—

If you could—ah but the moon's dead and the
    Clock's dead.
For we know now: we can give all
    But it won't do,
Not the day's length nor the black strength nor
    The blood's flush.
What we took once for a sure thing,
    For delight's right,
For the clear eve with its wild star in
    The sunset,
We would have back at the old
    Cost, at the old grief
And we beg love for the same pain—for a
    Last chance!
Then the god turns with a low
    Laugh (as the leaves hush)
But the eyes ice and there's no twice: the
    Benign gaze
Upon some woe but on ours no.
    And the leaves rush.

DECLINE AND FALL

We had a city also. Hand in hand
Wandered happy as travellers our own land.
Murmured in turn the hearsay of each stone
Or, where a legend faltered, lived our own.
The far-seen obelisk my father set
(Pinning two roads forever where they met)
Waved us in wandering circles, turned our tread
Where once morass engulfed that passionate head.

Cornice rose in ranges, rose so high
It saw no sky, that forum, but noon sky.
Marble shone like shallows; columns too
Streamed with cool light as rocks in breakers do.

O marble many-colored as reach of thought,
Tones so recollected and so distraught.
Golden: like swimmers when the August shore
Brightens their folklore poses more and more.
Or grey with silver: moon's whirling spell
Over the breathless olives we knew well;
Ivory as shoulders there that summer-dressed
Curve to come shyly naked, then find rest
(The tresses love dishevelled leaning dazed
And grateful). Or the wayward stone that blazed
As cheeks do. Or as eyes half-lowered flare.
Violet as veins are, love knows where.
Fine coral as the shy and wild tonguetip,
Undersea coral, rich as inner lip.

There was a stone to build on!

                         Friezes ran
In strong chorales that where they closed began;
And statues: each a wrung or ringing phrase
In the soul's passionate cadence of her days.

O stone so matched and massive, worked so well,
Who could believe it when the first brick fell?
Who could imagine the unlucky word
Would darken to the worldwide sigh we heard?
How our eyes wrenched together and held fast
Each face tightening to a chalky cast
(So poor a copy of one hour before).
Who could believe the gloom, the funnelled roar
Of cornice falling, forum falling, all
Falling? Or dream it fallen? Not a wall
With eaves to route the rain. The rivers swelled
Till roads groped in lakebottom. Nothing held
Clean edge or corner. Caking, the black flood
Left every luminous room tunnels of mud.
Earth shook: the columns walked, in midair clashed,
And the steep stone exploded as it crashed.

Soon the barbarian swarmed like locusts blown
Between the flood and spasm of our stone.
Grunted to tug their huts and marble sties
Where friezes broke like foam in the blue skies.
Blue noses poked, recoiling as they found
Our young and glad-eyed statues underground;
Singing salvation, the lewd chisel pecks
At boy and girl: one mutilated sex.

All our high moments cheapened—greed and grime
Charred them in rickety stithies to quicklime.

Murderous world. That town that seemed a star
Rose in our soul. And there the ruins are.
We'll not walk there again. Who'd wish to walk
Where the rats gather and grey tourists talk?
Who'd walk there even alive? Or bid his ghost
Trail phosphor on the melancholy coast?

POLONAISE

"Dobranoc, kochanie . . .
Pamiętaj o mnie jeszcze trochę . . ."

1.

The grey-green eyes, Polonia! then the bed
Throned with old trophies of a father dead.
Our star: a plane torn orange from the skies,
Szaro-zielone oczy, grey-green eyes.

Hair: bonfire gold the wind took. Blown amiss—
Half heaven lay blazing in the rain-swept kiss.
Rain taste of salt, kochanie? Cheek so cold
Under the sullen splendor, autumn gold?

Lips: in a candle's ardent trance. Or spoke
Rich in a dim significance of smoke.
Wine's lightning, lip to lip, harangued the heart:
Better the soul from body than lips part.

Sun princess, cinnamon-rose: when last we met
The panicky soldier ashen and a-sweat
Hefted his carbine, staring. Shadows close
Over a girl's defiance, cinnamon-rose.

But gardens of the breast, ecstatic still,
No passions empty and no passions fill.
No, though an eagle of Patmos warm her nest
Deep in a dole of roses, flowerbed breast.

2.

The flowering breast, Aneczka! still the dead
Vivid as poppies in the armored tread.
The east, a horde unshorn, the shaven west,
Loll in the half-track hooting, flowery breast.

Sun princess, cinnamon-rose: across your cheek
Mark of the darkness speaking when you speak?
Our willow, lovelock in the Vistula, knows
Dark of the moon becomes you, cinnamon-rose.

Hair, ember gold. Pan's tendril at the ear
Dusky with lovesongs of the darkening year.
Trains blunt as thunder, eye almighty, rolled
Over the gala shoulder, autumn gold.

Lips: in a candle's ardent trance. Or wine
Breathing Slavonian starlight in the pine.
At Biskupin—the enchanted cabins—start
Tales of the parted lips, the lips apart.

The grey-green eyes, rain-driven, fade afar.
What journey's end for children of the star?
Courage! He sings—great father—from the skies
Of szaro-zielone ever, grey-green eyes.

NOTE: The Polish phrase of line 4, translated by the words that follow it, is
pronounced rather like *sháh-doe zhe-láwn-eh áwe-chee*. Biskupin is an
ancient lake settlement in western Poland—one can still see remains of the
primitive huts in the marsh.

THE EVERGREEN

a.

Under this stone, what lies?
  A little boy's thistledown body.
How, on so light a child
  Gravel hefted and hurled?
Light? As a flower entwined
  In our shining arms. Heavy
Laid in this scale—it set
  Wailing the chains of the world.

b.

What did you say? We said:
    Bedtime, dear, forever.
Time to put out the light.
    Time for the eyes to close.
What did he do? He lay
    In a crazyquilt of fever.
His hands were already like grasses.
    His cheek already a rose.

c.

How was that year? His voice.
   Over sun on the rug, slow-turning,
Hung like a seabird lost the
   Lorn and bodiless cry.
Haunting the house. *And then?*
   I remember *then.* One morning
Silence like knives in the ear.
   A bird gone over the sea.

d.

What of his eyes? Dark glow
   Furling the world's great surface.
Bubbles among tree lights;
   Bubbles of ferny dew.
And his kiss? On our cheek at evening
   Vintage: a fine bursting.
This, and never dreamed his
   Span was a bubble too?

e.

Little head, little head,
  Frail in the air, gold aster—
Why did the great king stoop
  And smoothe those ringlets down?
For a tinsel party-hat?
  It was Christmas then, remember?
I remember grown men wept
  And couldn't lift that crown.

f.

Mother, these tears and tears?
   The better to see you, darling.
Mother, your golden glasses—
   Have a sorry fault,
Being made for things, dear,
   Mostly: carts and marbles.
Mothers wear, for children,
   Better the stinging salt.

g.

What you remember most—?
  Is a way of death with fingers.
How they are cast in tallow
  —Fingers, webbed as one.
Where was he going, with webs?
  A flying child? or a swimming?
He knew, where he went,
  One way back to the sun.

"Tesoro!" implored the maid.
　"Treasure!" the tall signora.
Under a distant heaven
　What struck the famous tower?
Faults in the earth despairing.
　Worlds away, an orchard
Offered violets early.
　And we returned a flower.

i.

Where does he lie? Hill-high
   In a vision of rolling river.
Where the dogwood curls in April
   And June is a dream of Greece.
Like a Christmas scene on china,
   Snow and the stubborn myrtle.
Those flakes from feathery heaven—?
   Deepen all in peace.

j.

Where does he rest, again?
  In a vision of rolling river.
What does he know of river?
  What do we know of sea?
Comfort?—when tomorrow's
  Cheek by jowl with never?
Never . . . in whose garden
  Bloomed the used-to-be.

k.

Under the snow, what lies?
    Treasure the hemlock covers—
Skysail of frost, and riding in
    Starlight keen and steep.
But the boy below? What's here is
    Gear in a sea-chest only.
Stowed for a season, then
    Pleasure-bound on the deep.

PARALLAX AT DJEBEL-MUTA

I

He strolled the desert cliff; tumultuous sunset
Drove a long shadow, phantom, over sands,
Honeycombed long ago—a thunder of granite
Teeters, pitching him down. Numb knees and hands

Gather beneath him; now he droops and rolls
Like a floored boxer his enormous head.
Ten feet above, a jagged edge of sky.
He had a flashlight; gropes, topples instead

Something that rocks like pottery; then the cool
Grooves of chromium fumbled-on in gloom.
Shadows—a black on sepia danse macabre—
Rage in a forty-century-old tomb.

Under an inch of dust, some rags and bone,
Rubble of royalty. The trained eye reads
Skulls of a boy and girl: his lank with fracture,
Hers in a constellation of blue beads.

Cinnamon, cassia, clove, mysterious such
Run from the tippy skull like hourglass sand:
The girl's hair caught close for windy riding,
A ruined cheek lagoons of lotus tanned,

And a whole shoulder by the broken bone
Nearly intact. El Greco lean. Stroked
By fingers shy as a new lover's it
Absently fell apart like ashes poked.

See the man hunched there? See his bleeding knee
Jostle the thirsty bone that, lacquered, dulls
Immediately like blotters? See him breathe
A stuff once sweeter, sounder than all bells?

II

Spring on the desert cliff: a wonder of sunrise
Fair on the chariot sporting Re, his disk
And halo of hooded snakes. Imported horses,
Plumes of flamingo and eye rolling, risk

A four-spoke bumping bronze wheel on the
    limestone
Lip of the gorge; the riders shout and lean:
She smiling, Nile-green eyes steady, golden
Throat and one shoulder bare. Do you think a queen?

Well his queen. Green pleats belted round his middle,
Shoulders armorial bronze, rein-sailing hand,
With falcon eyes half-shadowed on her, laughing,
Like skiers down and over the dazzling sand

Balancing paired—as for a season flesh
Glories, adoring any dare of soul.
Wide-circling, they rein in: sinew-corded
Burgeoning pillars by a ferny pool

Under two touselled palms: knotted sandals
Squeal in the padded sand; the lovers' lips
Explore at ease in their lost language, spelt with
Hawks looking hard at you, baboons and ships,

Bee, bittern, king of beasts, the crescent moon—
Flesh and blood alphabet. (Their flesh and blood,
So rich a drift on thornstock of the bone!)
—Even as they kiss, the ghost appeared, midflood

In sunlight, as in mingle of moonlight once
He came inspecting with archaic stare.
A rickety skeleton, gold-circled eyes,
Gold in his teeth, a wide skull without hair;

Left arm leathered to a prank of time;
Right, dry splinters, poking a chrome rod;
Before him buttons floating in air pit-patter
Castanets on his breastbone with each nod.

A breath of air his ruin. Teasing, they
Wheedle him near. Until lips radiant still
Panic the ghost. They, whistling their wild horses,
Sprang and like golden eagles took the hill.

ETRUSCAN TOMB

Tarchna dreams by the distant ocean—
Nobody knows how long a dream.
Sorts of lore
Old when the testy cardinal, blazing,
Ripped his sword from the heinous beam;
Old before:
Look, strange hordes on the bristling shore.
What a humus of tombs! and the ghosts and tokens
Storm like gulls at the furrowing team.

Time out of mind a ledge in a meadow
Nobody saw as heft of hands,
Rainy-grey,
Passed with a glance by the steely Romans
Frowning bigger and better plans—
Now, today,
Look, we have pried stone doors away!
What a burst of birds and frolic of dolphins
Swirling the air like banners and bands!

How they were drunk with hope, these children!
Nobody told them life was dour.
Gloomy tombs?
What, when tombs were salons for living!
Nothing had ended, that was sure.
Laurel blooms,
Look, in the bright, bird-flirting rooms.
What a chuckle of jugs, what crooning copper!
Flowers festooning the furniture!

And treasure catching the breath! in mines why
Nobody struck such eager wealth.
Oh no glow
Of morose ruby, viperous emerald
Here: here's candor and flush of health.
On this stone,
Look! what an outdoor field-fest thrown!
What a bright lense catching the dancers' passion,
Brow's abandon and barefoot stealth.

Horsemen flash on the sundrunk meadow—
Nobody drank so mad a sun,
Shoulders bold.
Eyes in rainbow of golden lashes
Laugh as the high-knee horses run.
Slick as coal,
Look! and the skyblue feyfoot foal!
What a hover of hooves like rippling fingers,
Manes that tangle and thunderous fun.

So friskily ferned and folked an ocean
Nobody sour of spirit knows.
Radiant haze
On the prism cliff and the waves that plop with
Lollop of dolphin springy as bows.
Bathers gaze,
Look, where the innocent fishline strays.
What a plunge from the reef as seabirds scatter!
Bodies simple as flowers unclose.

Though their tongue is a wild conundrum,
Nobody had such lucid hands:
Soothe or hoot,
Confer gently with troubled horses,
Reassure like a loving glance,
Cuddle fruit,
Look, and dazzle the twosome flute!
What a blur of birds! and the wingtip fingers!
Swallowy palms floating over the dance.

That dance! hips like a whisk of fingers;
Nobody had such flings of fun,
Flair as there!
No girl swung on a flank of satin,
None in a shiver of sequin spun
As these wear,
Look! pure limbs and halo of hair.
What a splendor of flesh! as if bones were breathing
Slender a fire as the virgin dawn.

Man's tomb—for the rest what greensick symbols.
Nobody else had lip so live,
Eye so fired.
Others mutter their maybes, pleading
Peacock, phoenix, and yew survive.
Tarchna choired
Look! what the soul itself desired.
What a mumble of skulls and dust from others.
All she sang was *Alive oh alive*.

Tarchna's death is a dive in sunlight.
Nobody knows how deep a dive—
See that sea!
Flung like sun in a seethe of rainbows
Drenched and laughing the dead arise!
Just to be
Look! in so wild bright brash a sea!
What a thunder of surf! and the great locks tossing.
Still she sang *Oh alive and alive.*

Tarchna's dark: in the bronzing twilight
Nobody treks the haunted run.
Broken loam
Scuffing the musk of age and autumn.
Westward, ah the effulgent zone.
Far below
Look! how the carmine harbors glow!
What a thrilling of red like brilliant music,
Like eyelids fast on a rapture of sun.

ROMAN LETTER

inventas aut qui vitam excoluere per artis
quique sui memores alios fecere merendo

What stormy barometers of emotion blown,
Upheaval in heaven, spells of moon and thunder
Over pediments piled to stupefy barbarians!
Odi et amo—girls of the region reaped a
Murderous wind: Rome's ornery as mortality.

Colossal oddments like a hollywood midden,
Lonely location of old superfilms.
How many a neighborhood in double exposure,
Epoch on epoch overthrust, outcropping;
Centuries telescoped like famous trains.

Look at the forum like old molars patched,
Clamps a-grapple and the bogus brick.
Deride if you will—but scuffing the chariot ruts
Of the Sacred Way, such panic of remembrance,
Such brunt of fact, delirium of old triumph
Thuds on the nape of your neck that reason reels.

Except for languor of the world's pretension,
The exhilarance of death and outer space,
Except for the platitudes in aquarelle,
Who'd love the stones of Rome—such brutal spoor
Tracking the verdigris and chalcedony?
The skull of the Colosseum, eaten clean,
(My charming American Daisy, Dublin Maud)

Eroded as old bone, dead as the moon—
What's the right tribute but the eye's aversion?

Remember the Lateran's gilded pugilist,
Thorax swollen like cobra's, cobra head,
Caligula's petted bullyboy?—there's your token.
Where else has propaganda such a pedigree?

It's hard to remember holiness was here
(Though never at home: was here with every horror
Of iron blurting red, of blood-soaked leather)
And left strange traces: a house of God, and aping
Some deified Julian's pool, some de luxe terminal?—
Bragging it's pure: no tourist with bare shoulders;
Bragging boisterously its big physique.

Sanctity's in the cellar yet. Those mines of
Silence and wild conundrum catch the breath.
Saints play at find-the-tomb: all's fabulous
The chisel chinks on here. Reach and rub wonder.

Shaken, reascend to the marble barns—
It's hard to forgive this temple! Best forget,
For Sant' Agnese, San Clemente, Quattro
Coronati, San Prassede's zodiac roof—
All reliquaries, a rapt jeweler's dream:
With God's great eye in jade, his hurricane hair,

His wrestlers and his virgins fierce as trees
Striving and staring where? Beyond. Their passion
Tugs at the world's inertia till it soars.

In Rome, encourage your eye to panorama,
Look far and wide; be chary of close looks
Where highfalutin pilasters weave, performing
St. Vitus' rites. (Cambodia's fevered stone
Is haunted so.) Never mind. We soon accept
As we accept the family bats in belfries,
The taints of a loved face. Come to require them
And wouldn't be without.

                    The face of Rome:
Imperial and autumnal, her remote
Blue eyes half-drowsed with multifarious loves,
Lips stirred voluptuously, the corners still
Triste with atrocities of long ago.
No queen perhaps—an actress all distraction
To men. A face to be milled in mellow gold.

Her color's gold. The color of cut melon
Gives succulence to any lean perspective.
Rome's all air and distance. Where is space
Such an impresario as here? So musical?
With water fluting from shells or plashing its palms
On rataplan troughs or timpani of water;
With air (from high Frascati or the sea's
Black-lava shore Tyrrhenian bathers hail)
A glossy talker in oriels of the laurel
Or tolling the tragic attitude of pines.

Pause on the brink of the Spanish Steps at evening
When the twilight-blooming youth, pale castaways,
Wash to that far-seen crag from every land,
And the schoolgirls swirl in their dirndls to sit
    like lotus;
Or stray on the Pincio redolent of the great
Great dead: look west to the Tiber and Monte Mario,
Where three domes in a row increase and hover
Like balls in a conjurer's palm.

An olio too mauve for candor of beauty,
Too flushed and mournful-eyed, with a trace of tremolo,
Yet here we'd live, and not for the saffron pergolas,
The picnic under the tomb in the Appian meadow—
But for prodigies and a cue or two, the pressure
Of many an atmosphere—all that impregnates
The pine by Egeria's water, the embosoming air.

FLORENCE

The yellow river and the violet hills
Henry James embossed in permanent-black
Jollied a flagging fellow to exuberance.
He saw the angel of Florence: cozy-gold.

This arrogant beauty soothe, who's least a flatterer?
Her suavity silk-on-steel; her ease ironic,
Queen of the pageant fox and panther lead.

On Bellosguardo's scarp (the intoning ghost
Our conscience and our quest; his cypresses
Leathery grenadiers for the lost causes)
Clamber the cobbled ramps in clarion air
To a gravel belvedere breezy and cedary
Lavishing:

　　　　Florence mortised in her hills,
Oxide-rose, a glory of quartz sunning.

Misnomer of blossomy nods, stern fleur-de-lys,
Igneous stone's your heritage and mood.

Over all, the ebullient dome, great brazen hub
Of the derelict circus-wheel of faith parading.
Michelangelo, off for Rome, raged at that cupola,
Eyelids hooding gruff energies of love:
"Excel her I cannot. Copy her—damned if I will!"

There's Florence to the core: those canyon spaces
Dry as adobe air, a sunset flush

Of memory burning where the glamorous name
Toppled, the weapon wedged in his skull, blonde hair
Sopped like a diver's: passionate Sandro spun
As panic rent the veil of the Mass; as blood
Wrote fast on the floor; Lorenzo behind portals
Paced tiger-thighed in rioting partisans,
Tear-spangled face a comet of imprecation.

Or the cotes of watery gold where Dante hefted
His sledge till the marble stung like spray!

                              Above,
How Giotto's mother-of-pearl recorder glories
Over tubas of cloud, over jubilant woodwind blue!

But listen: testy antiphons come wrangling
From the Palazzo Vecchio, haggard shawm.
Here's varmint-eyed, hard-bit, surly Firenze,
The snarl in the name, no name of blossoms now:
The hanged man's booted somersault from merlons;
Gullet stairs stilettoed bodies bump.

Duck with a sheepish cocktail under its turbulence,
Tourist in sporty shorts. The immense contempt
Of a truncheon torn from thorn, of fangy battlements,
Of a rusty-gold old hauberk-harsh façade
Panics your chattering camera to far corners,
Looms like an old bogy's matterhorn.
Compose its face to serene avatars,
Shrink it to atavism—not a flicker

From the craggy brows that rake Siena still
Through mountainous indigos of execration.

So to the river: yellow after showers
In quercine purlieus of the Casentine
Busy their taupe melodeons, clarabella.

Then Tuscan silt yaws cargoed to the sea.

She's a glum trawler then. But other mornings
Ply the sweet-minded mirrors.

                              Under the sunset
Her loitering dreamers, hunched toward Pisa, know
Dire aurum like the Arbia's: heinous red
You sniff in the wind still. What passion hangs
Over the ruined bridges! Underwater
The smoky palms of divers, webbed with mud,
Probe in lunging murk for the lost features.

Streets we essayed at every hour: those piquancies
Are graven deep in the brain—the nostril's tingle
At pine-shavings on pavements when the rain
Purpled the somber gorge of Vigna Nuova;
Or flower-banks under the granite mien, a sweetness
Coddled and mocked by dubious ambience:
Boisterous savor of hot herbs from kitchens;

Halls ether-sweet with desuetude; the celery
Reek in lichenous archways, iron-railed
Against such pungency: rankness of time,
Of human life and human love—its mouldering
Packed in the common halidoms we plod.

It's Rome for all cajolery. This Florence
You find in your own heart, if anywhere,
Prizers of wild acridity, sunset-crimson
Rancor of peach too near the rusty pit,
Or thralls of a northern calm, camellia-white
Of swimmers dripping from numb monochrome.

Surely no pendulous angel: cozy-gold.

O candor-of-almond cheek, cool lashes' raillery
Under the lancers' eave one drenching day,
Serene in the great hotel's flurry of foreigners,
Or niched from pitiless snow in San Frediano's
Grot of a door, by the bleak Bar's fluorescence,
Your hair a sowing of stars, oblivious lady—

From over time and the sea my gift, carissima.
Bear it with bantering palm: rough everlastings,
Thistles purple as stelliferous night.

REFLECTIONS IN VENICE

Except for the dowdy splash in back canals,
The lettuce and the lemon bold as brass,
All of that uppity ruckus on the radiant
Bayous dreaming of Byzantium yet,
Who'd ever assent to Venice? Who'd believe?

Men fancy pueblos so in the grand affair
Of a calliope sunset, see them plain
Through thirst over the witty sand's delirium.
Men have whimsies—but indulge them in marble?
Throw a bold roof on hallucination?
"Venice unseats the reason." Rather say
Reason became a delicate madman, chortled
Over preposterous blueprints. And approved them.
The daily bread's absurdity. What can never
Exist (for all of the bees in reason's bonnet)
You stub your toe on. The best leather scuffs.

Because the incredible's hourly and of course,
What takes the breath is wonder of banality:
The gondolier's shovelling shoulder, quirky wrist
(His long stroke like a billow tripped on shale)
Sculling not lovers but a bathtub, rags,
Mattresses, cabbage, or a coop with cacklers;
While over his sousing route one traffic light,
Alice's tabby—look!—appearing, disapp—

A straight line here?—anathema! Sobersided
Cities behave like waffles. Venice no.

Her gold palazzi ripple like theater curtains
When a door opens offstage on reality.
That Venice in the water, upside-down,
Is nearly as sound, as practical to live in.

Her skin: a great sea-creature hauled ashore,
Rind, hackle, hide and dewlap beached and fading
Under that glare from splendor of the depths
To grey of shale and pebble, of kelp sunning.

Watch how the walkers bob like kangaroo
Over the little bridges (pretty rickrack:
Wickets for the ancient sea disporting).
Streets are a crinkum-crankum, lithographed
Gameboard of Advance Three or Back to Start,
Left in a night of rain to bleach and frizzle.

What's for a prize? Ca' d'Oro: faded seine,
Her grey and coral plaited to catch time.
Opposite, in the fishmart, brooms of bracken
Scuffle the onion, orange-paper, sage.

What's for a prize? San Marco, malapert
To Parthenon-doting eyes: extravagant baggage!

A Cretan dancer on back somersault
Arching breast-up on ivory heel and finger.

At sunset, like a Valentine afire
That nick of time before it sags and blackens.

Tawny and sweet within, dark honeycomb
Of buckwheat shuffled with bright combs of clover.

Above, the dome's old glow—an artist's bowl
Where grime of gold was puddled till it crusted,
Left in a cupboard under cellar stairs
—A cat's eye in a jungle!—among cobwebs.

Hers is a floor, no, not to walk—to wade:
Lurching like sandbars under surf. Our weight
Thrills in the pitch and drag of seafloors drained,
The flora charmed, the osprey flat as fossils.

And the great souls that people the dark mountain!
Massing in fabulous funnies, fey charade.

Their gestures few as semaphores know poses.

Woe's a contusion, joy a vivid gash
On faces scored like boxers': chuck-full
Of rough conviction, nuggets in a gunny sack.

Where these parade, in stalagmite for toga,
The stone's alive: four-footed homes, pagodas
Shamble on pillar shank like headless pets.
All's neighborly: the houses men step out of
Crouch at their heel and sit there till commanded,

Handy as stools. The fishermen ease rumps
Into the cockleshells they're broader than.
All as it should be. These were made for mortals.

As mortals were for God. Why should great spirits
Fuss and truckle to pernickety blubber?
They've better things to con than right anatomy—
Eyes spellbound on the languorous green prince
Draped zigzag on his crisscross; on the angels
Gawky as new-hatched eagles from the shell;
On the great father's caving face of doom,
Beard like a snowslide in the Pyrenees.

Leaving the trance of northern night, go blinking
Into a blizzard of pigeons. Puzzle on it:
Venice, a shopworn rainbow. Maybe. But
In time's kaleidoscope what spunkier sparkle
As the great kingdoms pyramid and slip?
If man must have a single den, be denizen,
Venice would do. As well as Waffleopolis,
Suburbia's forty winks, or Little Wotting.

She'll set the wits a-tintinnabulating!

Restorative music in our time. And sovereign
For many a subtle canker. If it's granted
Our grief is of the heart or of the reason,
Settle in Venice, traveller—lose both.

A FRIEZE OF CUPIDS

Qui su l'arida schiena
Del formidabil monte
Sterminator Vesevo...

Pompeii: the seedy vendors
Ruffle and palm their books
Under the tourists'
Stirred or averted looks.

One gathers men loved women
Millenniums ago.
How, and how much? The tourists
Pay furtively to know.

Visions mauve and tender.
Scenes queasily sad:
The grey grit laid forever
Whatever bloom they had.

Lava composed their spirit.
Withered the wing of pride.
The mountain lapped these lovers
In a long side-by-side.

Our incest-ridden mumbler
Heard the great mother call—
His sick effusion dooming
The children one and all.

108

ORIGINATED IN A CHORUS
OF SATYRS

Had eager Eve for whose sweet will we languish,
Had Adam culled the garden as he should,
What of the great tale then: stone torso of anguish
Lost for the soft samoas of the wood?
Which of the three hurled *mawkish* at the florid
Dead-end of time? God's proxy manned to act?
Eve pondering palm on thigh? The Andean forehead
Blazing in clouds and lightning: *false to fact?*

Whose notion to explode the halcyon deadlock,
Dunging the garden with felicitous sin?
Harrow the native clay? Go clean to bedrock?
Which of the three hailed scathing vision in
When the eighth day made history?

                                     Pity and dread
Blazon like haloes the great blinded head.

ANCIENT OF DAYS

Spellbound as lunar buttes, the terrible past
Because it lies before me chills the bone.
In Knossos at high noon I mooned, dreamfast
On girls cartwheeling in sunflowers over the stone,
Schist or selenite. Or heard of worse:
Tar cocoons in earth the effendis sight
And syphoning in hot wax, tease back to birth
Ecce-homo's of lip-withering night.

Unless the opposable thumb (with crown and crozier:
Not pottering now in fields of Pleistocene)
Prove to our joy the pearly world's disposer
And not time's by-blow, as sucked craniums mean:—
Souls' saturnalia then! the moon's great gong
Enthralling the fairy pintos of the dawn!

AND A FORTUNE IN OLIVE OIL

Sweeten the moody world, Milesian waters,
Sparkle on Ur, on Lagash where it lies;
Drenching in dew the fertile crescent, scatter
The rosegold rumps babooning in the skies.
Flow to the squatting mother, nipples rigid,
Pupils of milkglass from the idiot sun,
Nursing her private Nile—over the turgid
Cats of the sand let freshets bubble and run

Rafting the first man ever to stand upright,
Ever through aqueous humor view the world,
Even its pyramids!—who (dared their true height)
Eyed the wide shadow on dominions hurled,
Bestriding his own: huffed gilas when he spoke
Ruptured like puffballs in irascible smoke.

AFFAIR AT THE FORK

The gods leaned forward at his bursting forth
Thick-booted out of Corinth, hating the business,
Hellbent for anywhere else. Rampaging north
(His face an icon of dust from the dim isthmus)
He clashed with foreigners where ruts contorted,
Glorying, "Room for the king of Corinth's son!"
High in the cart, an apparition snorted
And ground the hub on his leg—the sensitive one.

Damnation! Blind with pain, his temples pealing,
He wrestled the gauntface down, brow stunning brow,
Rolled savage among slaves, till passion cooling
Crooned for him tunes of decent headway now.
The gods sank back enchanted: flattering bell!
When had the fractious planet run so well?

CALLIOPE TO CLIO

μῆνιν ἄειδε, θεά, Πηληιάδεω Ἀχιλῆος
οὐλομένην, ἣ μυρί᾿ Ἀχαιοῖς ἄλγε᾿ ἔθηκε

The red wrath of Achilles—cope with that,
Muse, if you dare. Look doting on disaster:
Heroes dumped arsy-versy in hades' grot,
Lurid as lava pattering faster faster.
Flesh given to dogs—what bloomed in a queen's eye
Angry elastic snaggled in the fang;
And what the soaked crows spatter as they fly;
All this. Last, how the oxhorn lamina rang

As the lounging god (in profile to display
Better the measured nose, serene lip curling),
Called nonchalantly his targets, and let fly
With whinny of pleasure arrows cool as sterling.
That statue of him, though broken: the fine eye
Flicks unconcerned—why not?—the unnerving sky.

AGAMEMNON BEFORE TROY

Er will blos zeigen, wie es eigentlich gewesen—Ranke

A-traipsin' from a shindig, I unsaddles—
Three floozies an' a blatherin' buckaroo
Wangled the whole caboodle, and skedaddles.
You in cahoots with thet shebang, skidoo!—
Seein' if yer the critters I suspicion,
You varmints ain't a-goin' to hotfoot far.
Sartin galoots is sp'ilin' fer conniptions—
Wal, they's a posse hustlin' here an' thar

Fixin' to put the kibosh on shenanigans
By landin' scalawags in the calaboose.
Hornswoggled! sich palaver with bamboozlin'
Coyotes gits my dander up! Vamoose
Totin' spondulicks an' the cutie too!
They're itchin' fer a whangdang howdy-do!

ISHTAR

Two ordinary people, nextdoor neighbors—
Surely nothing for legend in these two:
He swishing in mint (his only labors)
Whirring matched irons over clover and dew.
And she for parties: the gold lighter poises
Shy in her fingers, an assyrian bird.
A downward smile, gilt sandals flexing. Voices
Curl in a pillowy corner, half unheard.

That night, the bedlamp fitful in her room;
Panes staring black and anxious. A race
Of lightning (thunder held, amassing doom)
Quivered long drenching seconds on each face.

Sweet firebird, fly away; fade, golden shoe.
Wait long and long, bright irons, for the dew.

A PRETTY DEVICE OF
THE FATHERS

A dagger (whose bone haft the iceberg locks)
Prime diamond in the nights of polar cold:
Sharpened by shamans haloed in white fox,
Their faces bland (obols of scythian gold)—
Butt fused in ice: the uncanny tool upstanding
Whetted so fine it sang in the least wind,
A glamor the grey lopers took to haunting,
Each eye a prickle of fire: wolves winter-thinned

Pad furry-eyed, tongues hankering for that bangle
(Bobbing like censers to the illustrious vault):
One runs a tongue along the edge: a tingle
Teases him, warm and sticky, thrilling of salt.
Delirious attar of life! The ecstatic glare
Glues them in furry carnage, sweet fangs bare.

NATIONE NON MORIBUS
(1265–1321)

... shrug off the world (as churning boys
  leather head tucked, shake tacklers and reel free)
  forgetting, just like that, the ingenious toys,
red hearts and yellow hair, the unstable quay,
  that tedium and Te Deum of our days,
  and with a mind clean as amnesia see:
the wanderer's double world, where intermaze
  (gold comb in gypsy hair) the event and vision:
  the Roman mouth its dark as copper phrase
long under dust, imperious with decision;
  woods hoarse and murky as unloading of coal,
  bitch-eyed libido in light air's derision—
    then, from the deck of planets as they roll
    to breathe that air! And breathless ... at the Pole ...

THE MIRROR

High holiday: the castle lank with banners
Swam like pagodas streamered undersea.
In gaudy gloom, rough honeycomb the casement;
Chink and rathole flash orfèvrerie.
By barbican or moat, in bramble shambling
The zany with his glittery smithereen,
Cutting the palm that fondles it—but catching
Cerise, cerulean, amber, grecian-green.

A hulker in the pitiless briar, a chuckler
Scuffing irascible honeybees of light.
The mirror shoots and cools. A briny iris
—Wandering wildfire of the outer night—
Cozily winks: a porcupine, that castle,
Spiny with fires that ravish and derange.
Lips flitter to the moon a rainbow spittle.
Cloudy as turning worlds the great eyes change:

Green with the misty liturgy, pale satin;
Roan where hairy forearms bang the board;
Quince with the leman fingers stealing thighward;
Gold where the black dwarf hunches—lo the lord!
Sheet-lightning eye, beard caracul as thunder,
Palms flickering dispensation, flaring wide
From twin tornado of purple sleeves; enthroned like
Genii of weather on the great divide.

The lord of rule and misrule, of the revels:
Outrager of fable in the sacred wood.
His image storms the oriels like voltage,
A maelstrom in the critter's pool of blood.
Who heard the one cry splintered among starlight?
Saw the moon-creature slump forevermore?
Not the fiesta-folk, whose dapper ceiling
Mirrors the ceiling mirrored in the floor.

When currents stir, and the blond soul of candles
Flees without giving ground, as dancers go,
When gusts in the wild arras plague the hunter,
His brow set deadly on the golden doe—
Only the weather eye avails up-current,
Sails by a ringlet drenched, a foundering light,
Home to that broken oak, to timbers giving
Under the weight of silence and the night.

THE NECROMANCERS

I

Clowns in a garish air. On panicky pedals
Managing monocycles for dear life.
And the heart pumps a ruby hoop—Fortuna's.
The princess flings our halo, knife by knife.

II

Tally the take in that affair with glory.
How I lay gaudy on the barbarous shore
Face burrowing in a patch of fern, blood stirring
Gamy as wines remembering summer stir.
No vein of all this flesh but leapt with memory:
Such splendor on lip and finger and the rest
As noon on a great range of sea, as heaven's
Moody amour, confusing east and west.

In grottos hung with cork and cordage bobbling
On halcyons where the lascar and his shade
Lay fecund in feluccas, hearts atumble
Made love a plague of angels, raving, unmade.

Deep comas of the sun! My loafing shoulder
Ached for the sweetness pillared on your palm.
Ear to the ground heard dusky tambours: *coming*.
A crackle of skirt, sails bantering with calm.
The weight of sweetness then! I saw it settle
(Curled on a whirling skirt) in my dark dream.

And jubilant: *honey and sun, the blood!* Music
Demurred from the warm dark: *inhuman stream!*

A voice from long ago. And the warm darkness
Shuddered how often on the barbarous shore
Since two defied, palms conjuring, a bayou
The bitterns boom adieu, and guard no more.

The wheel that fractured light has come full-circle.
Leans with the poky spoke dust deepens on.
Ours sang and singing died. But all one summer
Who knew for sure that wonder from the sun?

III

Clowns in a garish air. On panicky pedals
Managing monocycles for dear life.
And the heart pumps a ruby hoop—Fortuna's.
The princess flings our halo, knife by knife.

THE ACADEMY DISPORTING

In love with shadows all our days,
Creepers shunning dark and bright:
The dutiful, who troop to gaze
On friendship's long-exhausted rite;
To fob and shuffle palm to palm
Coppers of accustomed thought:
Decades have tested all we say;
And we lope roguish, as they taught.

Beneath the mistletoe will drift
Kisses the flat "punch" half warms.
Wan mirage of kisses. No
Likelihood of thunderstorms.
Compilers would look far to find
Milder perversities of lust.
There is no ruby in this ash:
Kisses that half stir the dust.

White shoulders we would press today—
Time is a great page torn between!
We nibble polite watercress
Fresher than memory, more green
Than Junes which gloated-over here
Would blast the many-eyebrowed room,
Alarming almost to its feet
The tableau stable as a tomb.

From where the soul with level look
Is hinting its contempt too well,
We flee—who cannot be alone—
Like bats poured panicky from hell.
From where the eye we dare not meet
Burns ruby in immortal bronze,
We break and run like giggling kids—
Ecstatic if a portal clangs.

Is there no lightning in the land
To show us, bitter black and white,
The car, the cottage, and the dune,
The hound a-howling all that night,
And where the imprudent, hand in hand,
Sway naked in immortal surf?
What vision haunts the summer land?
What wound is closing in the turf?

Shrimp on little picks impaled
Lie naked to the decent eye,
Grey frost their bed. Our fingers lift,
Insert them goggling, and put by—
Quashing a thunder in the soul
That rages to make all things right:
In love with shadows all our days,
Creepers shunning dark and bright.

THE CAVEMAN ON THE TRAIN

When first the apprizing eye and tongue that muttered
(Banished from Eden's air? Or pride of apes?)
Sat clinking flint on flint, and as they shattered
Snatched with a grin what fell in craftier shapes,
The law was move or die. Lively from tigers;
Dainty on deer. As weather called the tune.
Oxen, we learned, would bear us. So would rivers.
And that was science. On the whole a boon.

What caveman on a round rock dumped a-grunting
Rubbed at a rueful hip, brow darkening *why?*
Or gaped at boulders over gravel shifting
Until—a splendor of wheel-thought like sunrise!
No wonder: such example in a heaven
Revving immaculate gears, and at his feet
The planet on her axle greased and even.
Put any wheel to earth, and two wheels meet.

Athens cut ruts of marble; ivory courses
Caromed Apollo's car of talkative gold.
And Donne saw wagon-ways. The horsepower: horses.
Over the flats of Kansas sail-cars rolled.
First planks on querulous ground, then treads of metal,
Steel set edgewise, over stone for ties.
A mountain? Sawtooth rail or crank-and-cable
Till iron took serene the incredulous rise.

Compleat with a nifty moniker, *Puffing Billy,*
Best Friend of Charleston, Wabash Cannonball,
Cycloped (horse on treadmill trudging), dapper
Black and gold of Byzantium, *Sans Pareil*
Flew in the face of time and testy weather,
Enemies both, the lurid brakemen know.
(By stoves where sand is baking crisp, they gather
Trading the tall tales of high-striding snow.)

The lone prairie, the twilight grey as steel,
The vanishing freight—oh see the lonely road
Our fathers wandered, stumbling on the wheel
—Daydreamers all, and the long row unhoed—
Sky-hankering men, their reverence still alive
Some years ago: with burning glass and sun
George Stephenson in 1825
Snatched fire for *Locomotion No. 1.*

Ten miles an hour, "immoderate" twelve. Today
Slow Down to Ninety, warns the black ravine.

He will go far, the caveman, this-a-way.

By grand indifference to the red and green.

SPANISH BALLAD

¿Dó los mis amores, dó los?
¿Dó los andaré a buscar?

Rose and went a-roving, mother,
On the morning of St. John.
Rose and saw a lass a-laundering
On the ocean sands alone.
Lone she wrings and lone she rinses,
Lone extends them on a thorn,
All the while the clothes are sunning,
Sings a solitary song:

"Where's my darling, where, I wonder?
How to wander where he's gone?"

Up the ocean, down the ocean,
Still the girl goes singing on.
With a gold comb in her fingers
For her tresses ocean-blown.
"You, you sailor, tell me truly,
True as heaven steer you home,
Have you seen him pass, my darling,
Seen him faring on the foam?"

ISAIAH'S COAL

what more can man desire?

Always, he woke in those days
With a sense of treasure,
His heart a gayer glow
Than his window grand with sun,
As a child, its mind all whirring
With green and hollied pleasure
Wakes in a haze of *Christmas!*
The season of secrets done.

Or as one on country linen
Wakes with a start one morning—
Then on comfort snugger than pillows
Floats: July at the lake.
Or has married a golden girl
And can hardly believe, but turning
Sees blossom for him that very face
Worshipping cameras take.

Toy trains whirr perky on
Till springs contort beneath;
The middle-age rower slumps
Like a sack—indignant seizure!
Late editions wail
Screen Star in Mystery Death—
Yet in those same days
He woke with a sense of treasure.

Knowing: my love is safe
Though the Rockies plunge like water,
Though surf like a wildfire rage
And omens roam the sky;
Though limbs of the swimmer laze
Pale where the seaweed caught her,
Nothing can touch my love
As dangerous time goes by.

DE FIDE

Do you believe in Him? you ask. Safer to say No,
Since what I'd be admitting could be a death of snow,
Some hatchet whacks on an old log where pigmies
    slit the skin,
A Moses-beard, tremendous crag, or formulas of wind.
To these and maybe yours, it's No. But for another
    there—
You'd wonder, when I fill my lungs: Do you
    believe in air?

LAST JUDGMENT

When we are ranged on the great plain of
   flabbergasting death,
Feeding (for our lungs hang slack) on air not drawn
   with breath,
And see, for many miles around, our Easter Island lie,
The gaping dumbshow of our shame, in footlights
   from the sky:
How many a scene long out of mind in rooms we
   barely knew,
Punch amok or Judy lewd, lit fuchsia-red or blue,
And see our working face in each and sway a
   moment numb—
Then save us from our rage Yourself; let lightning
   cry our doom!
Having such motive for their hate, each knowing
   what it knows—
We know our terrible hearts too well to trust our
   luck with those.

THE IVY AND THE RUNE

i.

They whitened at the privilege
Of tiptoeing near death
To watch his fingers skeining
Hand over hand the breath

From lips like violets blanching—
This taught a thing or two.
Their palms were mute; their faces
The shape of what they knew:

Something of love, whose eyes burn
Gayer with failing breath;
Of flesh, a dull conductor
Of nearly all but death.

Knowing, they shrunk closer
(The deadened with the dead)
When night drained of color
Drowsy aster-head.

Through that wound, the world lay
In extremis too:
Meadows wailed their mossy blood;
Heaven bled its blue.

ii.

"This flesh, a toy of death;
His cat-and-mouse display.
Tomorrow's numbing fall
Tense in the air today.

"A crazy frame, soon down,"
I grieved. But Love said, "Look!"
And the flesh soared and such
Wonderment took;

The eye so fine a star,
The cheek such mains of light
That "O Love, you appear
Unendurably bright!"

The sky glowed softly, "I?"
And marvelling, "*I* appear?"
Then all midheaven shone: "I
But set a finger here."

iii.

The rose cajoling, "Now?"
The moon with shapely "Here?"
Persuaded. Waved away
The sheriff face of fear

Hardening, "Easy! *Here's*
Bad acreage of *Where*.
And *Now*'s a fool mirage
Over coyote air."

"No, *Here*'s the attractive moon."
(The sheriff whacked his star.)
"And *Now*'s a garden dial
Where affluent roses are."

So once. No roses now.
No moon's ill-gotten glow.
Here shivers, "Far away?"
And *Now* weeps, "Long ago."

CONCLUSION

legato con amore in un volume
ciò che per l'universo si squaderna ...

If what began (look far and wide) will end:
This lava globe huddle and freeze, its core
Brittle with cold, or pulled too near its friend
Pop once like one gun in a long-drawn war,
And the stars sputter one by one, the night
So empty judging *empty*'s out of date
(Space and time gone), then only, height on height,
Mind that impelled those currents and that freight,
Mind that after five days (see those days!
Regions all tropic one day, one all ice!)
Whistled man from the sea-moss, saw him raise
The blundering forepaw, blink from shaggy eyes—
If image, likeness in the ox-yoke brow
Long out of focus, focused mind to Mind—
Ah what unspeakable two and two allows
That silence huddle and all eyes go blind?
Our ups and downs—there! that remembered makes
Memory which is the single mind. How sweet
Carmine stars of the maple fumed in rakes
At 1350 such and such a street.
A thing to keep in mind. Yes and keep yet
When the vile essence violescence lies.
Once in winter by the richening sill
Quiet, the fireplace tiny in our eyes—
I mention this; there's more. The Almighty will
Aeons late stumble on it with surprise.

FROM

OF FLESH
AND BONE

FEW THINGS TO SAY

It's true, we write so little. Years between
Words in this, that, or the other magazine.
Few things to say—two maybe. Girls, know why?
You craze the air with pleasure. And you die.

BIKINI

The naked flesh brings tears: the ways so few
For love to enter. And its quick adieu.
Death, the cold ogler, shrugs—by many a way
Comes when the whim is on him. Comes to stay.

CAPE ANN

You bathers where the stinging sprays are blown,
Ponder your flesh, its queries on the bone.
A question mark, the calf. Thigh and yes there!—
Ponder the fond interrogations. Tear
Your gaze away to the spine's aplomb, rainbow
At shoulder. And flourish of hair, a jaunty "So?"
In teeth of the wind.
     From time's old slapdash chasm
What drew (to abash the sky) that curious plasm?

THE GIRL

Toe testing ocean, on the starlit sands
—Her body like brilliant reasoning—she stands;
And, blown with the blowing dark about her face,
Streamers (like fields of force from outer space),
Streamers: her love, grief, memory seem that tree
The northern lights shake glittering. Could we see,
We'd see all heaven cartooned, all myth aglow,
See nebulae shiver as she dips a toe.

AT DAWN

"Living!" I grieved. "Each heartbeat, touch-and-go."
Sleepy, you touch and grin: "What touches, though!"

DAYS OF OUR YEARS

It's brief and bright, dear children; bright and brief.
Delight's the lightning; the long thunder's grief.

YEARS LATER

Good-byes were easy, with a casual hand.
But who, years later in a darkening land,
Seeing another with that same pale skin,
Fought with his heart to choke the blind tears in?

ANACREON'S ANSWER

"No sense of age? These white hairs on your head,
You take this gold and pink thing to your bed?"
 Of age? For men, two sorts alone are doled:
 The dead years. The alive years, white or gold.
 I and the pink thing are alive-years-old.

LOVE AND DEATH

And yet a kiss (like blubber)'d blur and slip,
Without the assuring skull beneath the lip.

WITH FINGERING HAND

Goethe, *Römische Elegien*, 5, 16

Ten thousand cigarettes from now,
  As many drinks away,
I may forget—"O honey, hush!
  Let sleeping lovers lay."
Let sleeping lovers *lie,* my dear.
  "I know as well as you.
But here's a love that's out for rhyme.
  Can't even that be true?"

CONCEIT

So, with one burning word from you
  Again the glacier came?
And where you set so cool a foot
  The world went up in flame?

"Now what a way to say you're cross
  But love me just the same!"

RHETORIC

Some two decades, dear, apart,
Keep it shy, the younger heart?
Never mind. Some others passed
Bring us to one room at last.
Forty years we toss in two;
Forty thousand are too few
For the last triumphant bed—

"Hush and love me, winterhead!"

MATHEMATICS

On your own flesh these fingers (once all thumbs),
My gold and ivory abacus, learned their sums.
The more I mused, the more assurance grew
What's loveliest, love, comes only *one*, or *two*.
Though some call *seven* holy, and some *three*,
I found no sevenish thing, no trinity.
Long at wit's end I wondered, *This?* or *this?*
Till all our *two*'s came single in the kiss.

FOLK SONG

May your flesh and its pleasant assembly delight
The many by day, but one only at night.
   "One only, my only, if only that one
   Would not look so broad by the girl-flushing sun."
Clay pigeons! I test me on every fine mark,
The better to find you, my dove, in the dark.
   "The better to lose me. Loose shooter, take heed.
   My pleasant assembly a bull's-eye indeed!"

PROTESTATION

"You say so, but will you be faithful? You men!"
But dear, I've been faithful again and again!

PARTING

"We met in error. If too close,
   Regrets. And I'm away.
Yesterday was easy come;
   Easy go, today.
Forget the way we burned, we two,
   That pain on either part.
Forget we fell convulsed as one."

   Said knifeblade to the heart.

GOSPEL

Fresh from another's bed, that kiss for me?
Here's generous flesh, my dear? Soul's charity?
Or is the poor head puzzled? Good words run
Love one another. Not: *another one.*

CONTEMPLATION

"I'm Mark's alone!" you swore. Given cause to
   doubt you,
I think less of you, dear. But more about you.

ON LIGHTING HER CIGARETTE

Helen, the tiny fire my fingers cup
Close to your breath—be careful. Don't look up.
Small gaudy fierce, it serves. But given a chance
Sheets of flame catch you in the tragic dance.

LOVE

"For when we have blamed the wind, we can
    blame love."
Who'd blame the mindless wind? Sleepers that start
In fear when the ceilings heave like seas above?
Girls with their shattered dresden in the heart?

NATURE LOVER

Some look at nature for the surface: eye
Vetch, vireo, pond with willow, wandering sky.
Dealers in scenery, no? Obscene as those
Who looking at a girl see only clothes.

BLIND JOY

Crude seeing's all our joy: could we discern
The cold dark infinite vast where atoms burn
—Lone suns—in flesh, our treasure and our play,
Who'd dare to breathe this fern-thick bird-rich day?

VISION

That blonde! waves lapping over rod and cone.
What glee in this amorous gadget, flesh and bone!

MEMENTO

The flesh says: "Finish. I'm not long for you.
Tomorrow to another. And soon due
In ferns. Or on a gull's salt feather flown.
Or finswept shoalward. Finish. I'm a loan."

EMBROIDERY AT BAYEUX

Men fought with axes, panting, nose to nose.
Women with pretty stitches pictured those.
The severed head lies beaming, "I'm a rose!"

TRANSPLANT

When I've outlived three plastic hearts, or four,
Another's kidneys, corneas *(beep!)*, with more
Unmentionable rubber, nylon, such—
And when *(beep!)* in a steel drawer (DO NOT TOUCH!),
Mere brain cells in a saline wash, I thrive
With thousands, taped to quaver out, "Alive!"—
God grant that steel two wee *(beep!)* eyes of glass
To glitter wicked when the nurses pass.

VIEW FROM MOON

Once on the gritty moon (burnt earth hung far
In the black, rhinestone sky—lopsided star),
Two gadgets, with great fishbowls for a head,
Feet clubbed, hips loaded, shoulders bent. She said,
"Fantasies haunt me. A green garden. Two
Lovers aglow in flesh. The pools so blue!"
He whirrs with masculine pity, "Can't forget
Old superstitions? The earth-legend yet?"

146

MINOTAUR

Sweet flesh was shipped the bull-man once to eat.
You think it's changed, you children on the street?
Go home and pack. Tomorrow, off for Crete.

PHILOSOPHER

He scowled at the barometer: "Will it rain?"
None heard, with all that pattering on the pane.

PASTORAL

Once Cruddy in the countryside
Touched poison ivy. And it died.

AVANT-GARDE

"A dead tradition! Hollow shell!
Outworn, outmoded—time it fell.
Let's make it new. Rebel! Rebel!"
Said cancer-cell to cancer-cell.

VISITING POET

"The famous bard, he comes! The vision nears!"
Now heaven protect your booze. Your wife. Your ears.

PRIZES, ETC.

Honors corrupt the blood. Disturb like gin.
We squirm being flattered, cringe being told,
   "You're in!
About your brow the immortal auras glow!"
Liar! I sniff the festering blood below.

EPITAPH FOR A POET

Let chips of marble fly, and chisel chime:
His life was meager, but his song sublime.

"His song was *what?*" You heard me. For the rhyme.

EPITAPH FOR A LIGHT LADY

Once, lovely Chloe here asleep in clay
Warmed with warm flesh whatever place she lay.
And now so long abed, yet cold as stone?
And—so unlike our Chloe—sleep alone?

ANOTHER

The whole world takes her to its bed below.
As she took all the world. Or nearly so.

IN DARK OF NIGHT

I see you, love, in your low home
The night-things comb. And catacomb.
"A sort of trash, the body." No:
Good sticks to set the soul aglow.
"Good sticks?" In dark of midnight, think:
To brighten truth, we blacken ink.
"Mere image!" God's Quijote swore
The passionate bed's mere metaphor.

PEOPLE ON BUS

How all these cheeks a-twitch, loose, dumpy, dull,
Long for the echoing splendors of the skull.

SOPHOMORE

Last year I'd tease, "So beautiful! So dumb?"
She'd laugh "I guess," and let the tears half come.
"Confuse such easy lines?" "I tried and tried!"
"Julie, you moon at school. All dreamy-eyed!"
　　So last year. Now, as girls lie on the sand
　　In summer, hair flung over cheek on hand,
　　She—by the curb, in pink of flares. Poor head,
　　Lost in your dreams? Confuse *Early to bed?*

ON THE ONE THEME STILL

In traffic shuddering as it shied too near
That tumble of lovelocks at the silent ear,
She lay, outstretched as if for pleasure, more
Languid than any girl on any shore.
Love taught the pose. *Such cronies, love and death?*
Old bosom friends. If differing, by a breath.

GHOST

Night by night the bony mesh
Slumbered in its bed of flesh.
Now the bone, turned out of bed,
Wanders the wide night instead.
Not a miser picks at gold
As these shabby nails the mold.
Ah, to patch it, shank and girth,
There's not earth enough on earth.

THE VISIT

I loved a girl. She died. I stood here, so;
Stared at the something strangers put below.
Again I stand a moment. Not to stay.
Evenings she'd tease, "Don't wait if I'm away."

LOVERS

And here the two by the one grievance haunted
Lie in the dark. But not the dark they wanted.

PERFECT RHYME

Life, that struck up his cocky tune with *breath*,
Finds, to conclude in music, only *death*.

151

ACKNOWLEDGMENTS

"Christmas" reprinted with permission of America Press, Inc. © 1949. All rights reserved.

"At Dawn," "Days of Our Years," "Love and Death," "Philosopher," "The Visit," and "Lovers" reprinted with permission from the May 1967 issue of the *Atlantic Monthly*.

"Few Things to Say," "Years Later," and "Minotaur" reprinted with permission from *Chicago Sun-Times Panorama*, 8 April 1967.

"City Dawn," "The Indolent Day," "Human Kind Cannot Bear Very Much Reality," "Isaiah's Coal," "Blind Joy," and "Memento" reprinted with permission from *Commonweal*.

"Portrait" and "The Weeds" reprinted with permission from *Harper's*. Copyright 1948 and 1949. "The Child" was originally published in *Harper's* under the title "For My Son." Copyright 1949.

"Watcher Go Deftly" and "Winter in the Park" originally appeared in the *Kenyon Review*, vol. 12, no. 1 (Winter 1950).

"Parting" and "Embroidery at Bayeux" reprinted with permission from the *Nation*.

"Contemplation" first appeared under the title "A Thought for Tristram" in *The New Yorker*. © 1967 by The New Yorker Magazine, Inc.

"Magazine Stand" reprinted with permission from *Partisan Review*. Copyright 1943 by Partisan Review.

The following poems first appeared in *Poetry* and are reprinted with permission: "Love Poem," "Aftersong," "The Masque of Blackness," "Fairy Tale for Marion," "Old River Road," "The Young Ionia," "Decline and Fall," "Etruscan Tomb," "Florence," "Parallax at Djebel-Muta," "Ishtar," "Conclusion," "Dollar Bill," "Penny Arcade," and "Parting: 1940."

"Originated in a Chorus of Satyrs" and "Ancient of Days" reprinted with permission from *Prairie Schooner*. © 1958 by the University of Nebraska Press.

The following poems were first published in the *Saturday Review:* "Train-wrecked Soldiers," "Midwest," "Foto-Sonnets," "With Fingering Hand," "Gospel," "Epitaph for a Light Lady," "Transplant," which appeared under the title "D.O.M., A.D. 2167," and "View from Moon," which appeared under the title "A.D. 2267."

"Roman Letter" and "The Lover" were first published in the *Sewanee Review*, vol. 65, no. 2 (Spring 1957) and vol. 67, no. 4 (Autumn 1959). © 1957 and 1959 by The University of the South. Reprinted with the permission of the editor.

"A Pretty Device of the Fathers" reprinted with permission from the *Virginia Quarterly Review*, Autumn 1958.

"Polonaise" and "Last Judgment" reprinted with permission from the *Times Literary Supplement*.

"Folk Song" and "Ghost" originally appeared in *TriQuarterly*. © 1968 by TriQuarterly. Reprinted by permission.